Wind Shadow WEST

The sloop Wind Shadow *departs home port, California's Channel Islands Harbor, on a pre-voyage shakedown cruise. The author is at the helm (photograph by Ed Matisoff).*

Wind Shadow WEST

Ralph J. Naranjo

Hearst Marine Books   NEW YORK   1983

Library of Congress Catalog Card Number: 83-81660

ISBN: 0-688-02508-0

Printed in the United States of America

First Edition

1 2 3 4 5 6 7 8 9 10

Book Design by Maria Epes

To Lenore with whom I shared a fantasy &
To Tara and Eric with whom we shared the world

Preface

Moving aboard and moving ashore established the time limits of our cruising way of life. It was a sailing alternative spanning six years and the world's three greatest oceans. With the thorough change in life-style came changes in our values. The years aboard *Wind Shadow* were neither an extended vacation nor an overindulgence in recreation. They were a commitment to a shared interest that grew into a viable way of life.

The rewards were numerous. The traumas remain vivid. We sailed away from suburbia as a family, crossed oceans, and returned with new perspectives. We learned to feel the weather, anchor securely, and look more closely at what there was to see.

Crossing lonely oceans in a small sloop with a short-handed crew can be a folly or a fantasy realized. New freedoms are tempered with additional responsibilities. The concept of selling everything and sailing away is not original. For those who make the proper preparations, develop the necessary seamanship, and master the art of navigation the sea holds many rewards.

Snow now covers the shoreline of Oyster Bay. *Wind Shadow* lies dormant . . . stripped of spars, engine, and bottom paint. It is time to refit the vessel and reevaluate our experiences. From our cottage window I can see our sloop, the ice-covered bay, and the boatyard I am involved with. At times the memories of Polynesia seem too distant and I question how long a sailor can remain ashore.

This book was written for those who dream of getting away as well as for those who are ready to go.

—RALPH J. NARANJO

Oyster Bay, New York, 1983

Acknowledgments

This book evolved from feelings about the sea, a vessel, and the sharing of experiences as a family. Without the help of the following hardy souls, our voyage in *Wind Shadow* might have left us with markedly different memories.

Tony Babich (*New Zealand*)
Yves Betuel (*Mauritius*)
Denis and Eva Brown (*New Zealand*)
Colin Busch (*New Zealand*)
Alistair and Davina Campbell (*South Africa*)
Karen D. Cardamone (*U.S.A.*)
Helen Dempewolff (*U.S.A.*)
Lawrence and Herberta Dempewolff (*U.S.A.*)
Richard and Rita Dempewolff (*U.S.A.*)
Tom Doyle (*U.S.A.*)
Father George (*Cook Islands*)
Christine Hall (*New Zealand*)
Lex and Jill Lundmark (*New Zealand*)
Charles E. Mason (*U.S.A.*)
Lee and Anna Lee Matthews (*U.S.A.*)
Brother James McGrath (*U.S.A.–Fiji*)
Micky McTeague (*U.S.A.*)
Bob and Edith Melrose (*U.S.A.*)
Ross and Minine Norgrove (*U.S.A./New Zealand*)

➤ 9

Wind Shadow WEST

Tony and Val Pierce (*New Zealand/England*)
Jerry Schudda (*U.S.A.*)
John and Olive Shanks (*New Zealand*)
Morris Weber (*U.S.A.*)
John Whiting (*U.S.A.*)
Chris Wulff (*Australia*)

Contents

Preface   7

Acknowledgments   9

Chapter 1   Getting Started   17

Chapter 2   First Passage—Hawaii and the Pacific   35

Chapter 3   Polynesia   61

Chapter 4   New Zealand and Australia   85

Chapter 5   Navigation and Seamanship   113

Chapter 6   Special Experiences—
             South Africa and the Indian Ocean   129

Chapter 7   Tara and Eric   149

Chapter 8   When It's Over   171

Appendix A   Other Passage Makers   189

Appendix B   *Wind Shadow*—Hull, Rigging, and Gear   191

Wind Shadow WEST

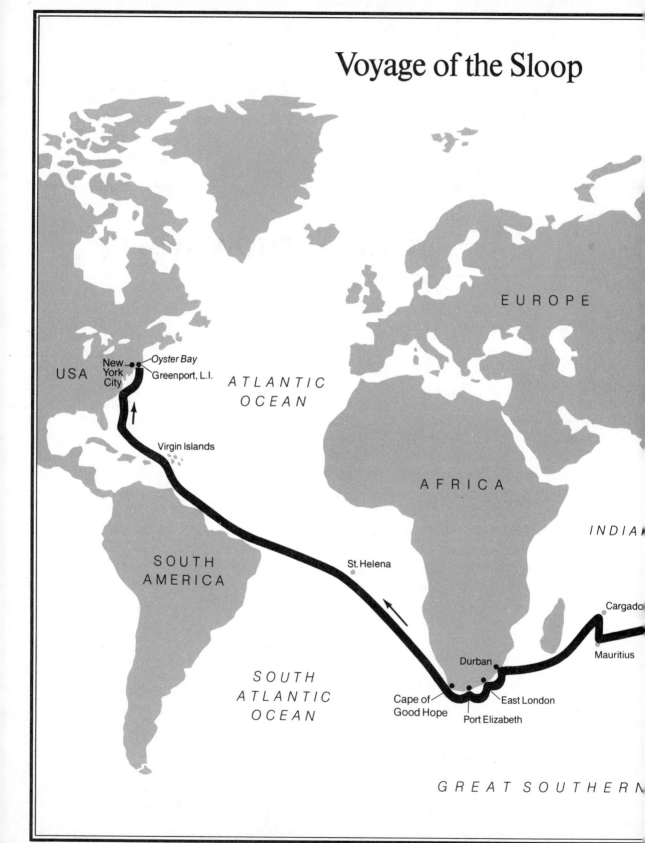

Voyage of the Sloop

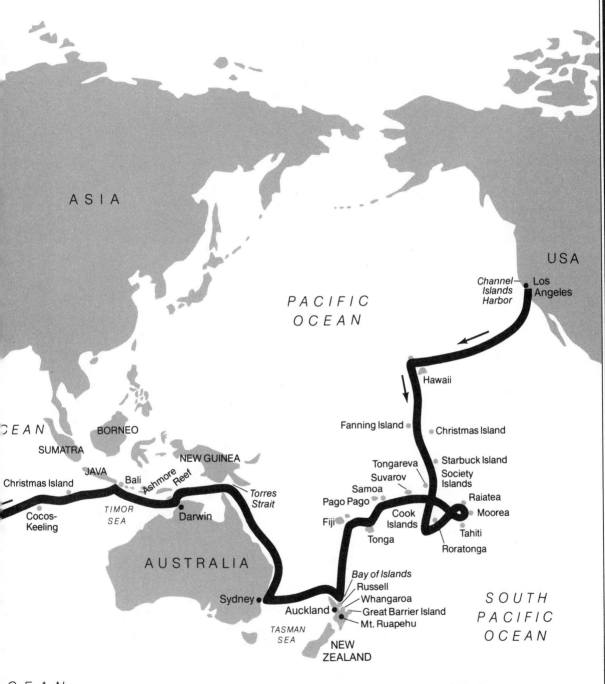

Wind Shadow (1976-1980)

CHAPTER 1

Getting Started

The setting moon revealed a clear horizon. Easterly trade winds remained steady, not gusty, and the seas were long and rolling. My wife Lenore and our two children Tara and Eric, age seven and nine, were asleep below. A squall seemed unlikely. Occasionally porpoises broke the surface near the stern. It was about 0300 on August 22, 1979. We were in the middle of the Timor Sea, 1,150 days along in what would be a five-year journey. It was a good time to indulge in the pure pleasure of sailing.

I disengaged the self-steering gear and took the helm by choice rather than by necessity. Seas large enough to lift *Wind Shadow's* stern, yet soft enough to be of little concern, rushed by. The steeper ones added a bit of surfing to the excitement of sailing a trade wind reach. At times, the bow wave frothed its way aft, the hull cleaving a trench in the sea. Eventually the sky in the east hinted of dawn and I was reminded of navigational responsibilities. It was time to take a round of star sights and watch a new day unfold.

The sounds of dolphins awakened the crew. Tara and Eric hurried to the rail to trade glances with friends. Porpoises always made them happy. Perhaps it had something to do with the joy that these animals conveyed through their mastery of the sea. Their acrobatic repertoire had been learned in the remote stretches of the Great Southern Ocean. Their greeting set the tone of the day.

The conditions we had encountered between Bali and Christmas Island, south of Java in the Indian Ocean, were too good to be taken for granted. Being at sea, even in the trade wind latitudes, is usually a mixture of

Wind Shadow rushes along under staysail and storm trysail—in one of the gales that infrequently alter the calm trade wind routine.

moods. Some days are comfortable; others are not. Sunshine, flying fish, and exhilarating sailing are part of the good-day stereotype and typified our entry into the Indian Ocean. Sailors are superstitious and I began to worry about too much sunshine. It was in fact a prelude to something very different. About a thousand miles to the west, the Indian Ocean would balance the account. For the moment, however, our forty-one-foot sloop and the vast sea were in phase, and the crew was happy.

By mid-morning a sunny-day routine had been established. Tara was curled up on deck in the shade of the mainsail. All of her concentration was focused on the book in her hand. Eric had been bribed with some treats from the galley into a somewhat enthusiastic approach toward his correspondence school lessons. Even so, his real interest lay in his sister's updates on the adventures of *The Hobbit* heroes she was reading about. I couldn't blame Eric, for the siege of the Dark Tower seemed infinitely more appealing than his search for simple predicates.

Lenore was on deck checking sail trim and self-steering gear adjustment. I had assumed my favorite off-watch position and was preparing for a lengthy nap. Just as I fell asleep, I heard my wife say, "Have you seen how exposed the anchorage at Christmas Island is?" She knew she had gained my attention, but just to be sure she added, "The holding ground doesn't look too good either."

The nap was sidelined and we proceeded to look over charts, *Admiralty Sailing Directions*, and a letter a friend had written describing the island. After some serious speculation we agreed that although the island was open to the west, it provided a good lee during the trade wind season. The predominately coral bottom would not pose a problem to our all-chain anchor rode. Satisfied that we understood what surprises lay ahead, Lenore turned her attention to Eric's grammar lesson and I opted for a leeward berth and a chance to regain nap status.

The sound of the sea lapping on the hull left me wide awake. It reminded me that there was about one inch of fiberglass laminate between the crew of *Wind Shadow*—my family—and an ocean over three miles deep. From time to time, of course, every sailor thinks of the gambles taken. Perceived dangers and rewards must be evaluated. An explanation of why we chose such an alternative takes us from the good sailing we

➤ 19

found in the eastern Indian Ocean and back to years earlier and halfway around the world, to where it all began.

Today the window in front of me overlooks Cold Spring Harbor, New York. It is the bay where my water thoughts originated, where I first shared them with my wife, and where we concluded a voyage across three oceans. I was about ten years old when the sidetracking began. Disappointed over an inability to play little league baseball, I turned my attention toward a plywood skiff and a pair of spruce oars. Bronze oarlocks made encouraging sounds and my priorities were refocused upon my boat, the bay, and the things they introduced to me. Summer was what I waited for. Many of my friends succumbed to late-August blues and spoke of getting back to school. I never shared such a feeling. If there are different drummers, I must have followed the pied piper.

Over the years my interests in water activities broadened. Fishing, waterskiing, sailing, diving, and surfing added different perspectives. They also fostered skills that would later be clear assets.

Lenore sampled family boating with her parents and sisters, who each summer made their way along the South Shore of Long Island, through Moriches Bay and the Shinnecock Canal, and into Gardiner's Bay. Her memories are filled with recollections of quiet anchorages, dinghy rowing, and learning to swim. These early times on the water surely helped her welcome cruising life.

Lenore and I moved to California in 1968, enticed by a year-round boating season. At first daysailing and dinghy racing were just another kind of water interest for us. But the nearby Santa Barbara Channel Islands changed our perspectives. Our first cruising boat, a twenty-six-foot Excalibur sloop named *Intuition*, altered our priorities. Weekend cruises and vacation voyages introduced us to family sailing. Our children were still in diapers. Nonetheless, our mini-cruises combined many of our interests in a package hard to beat.

Intuition was a modern production sloop with simplicity engineered into every aspect of her design and construction. Cabin accommodations were minimal. She had V-berths forward and two settee berths in the main saloon. A sink and simple one-burner alcohol stove were the rudiments of a galley. Her hull and cabin were in proportion to each other. Designer

Channel Islands Harbor, home port for both Intuition *and* Wind Shadow, *has a year-round boating season and a welcome nearness to islands for weekend cruising.*

Bill Crealock had made no effort to place the living space of a thirty-two-footer into the compact twenty-six-foot hull. Fiberglass, teak, and stainless steel kept maintenance to a minimum. We learned about the assets and shortcomings of these materials and opted for the same in *Wind Shadow*.

Our years of coastal cruising were filled with new experiences. Occasionally fog, large swells, or an infrequent cold front emphasized the importance of good navigation and seamanship. Enjoyable sailing, spring wild flowers, and solitude linger as memories of the Santa Barbara Channel Islands.

During the summers of the late sixties and early seventies we interspersed cruising with camping. Summer vacations included several journeys across the country in a VW van. Winter vacations became a time for travels into Mexico. We explored arid beaches and jungle rivers. Baja was traversed before the tourist road was built. Aboard our van we carried surfboards, fishing poles, camera gear, and an Avon dinghy. Our interest in unscathed natural places continued to grow. I remember the days spent in our van in Bahia Concepción—especially the one when a small sloop arrived. I wondered what it would be like to be aboard *Intuition* in a similar setting.

Before long, plans began to evolve. Instead of Mexico I substituted a passage west to Hawaii. Two close friends volunteered as crew. Preparations for the 2,300-mile voyage began. Jerry Schudda and John Cort had very little sailing experience, but both were well-disciplined outdoorsmen.

For months we prepared for the passage to Hawaii. Jerry and John sailed aboard *Intuition* regularly. Since space was limited, gear was selected carefully. Acquaintances who had made the passage before us volunteered valuable information. On July 3, 1974, *Intuition* slipped through the breakwater of Channel Islands Harbor and out into the open Pacific. Her crew was rightfully apprehensive.

Nothing wakes a sleeping sailor as quickly as impending disaster. It struck as we approached the midpoint of our passage, twelve days out from Channel Islands Harbor. The night had been overcast and moonless. Jerry was about to turn the watch over to John. A cry of concern woke me. The first words I heard were, "We're sinking!" Rolling out of my berth, I splashed into water nearly a foot above the cabin sole.

Instinctively I groped through the bilge, checking for the source of the leak. The answer was close at hand: a cockpit drain hose had parted well below the waterline. Luckily I had functional seacocks on all through-hull fittings and could quickly shut off the incoming stream.

The danger was far from over. We had taken on so much water that *Intuition*'s motion caused it to surge fore and aft. The change in weight and trim caused her to alter her steering characteristics drastically. If we dropped sail the cresting trade wind seas could easily overwhelm us. Broaching at the wrong time could mean being swamped by breaking seas.

John and Jerry started in bailing. The next hour at the helm seemed an eternity, but finally the bilge was dry and the worry of further catastrophe subsided.

The next morning we took stock of the damage. Many of our packaged stores had been destroyed by the water. It was the least of our worries. We had ample food for our extremely marginal appetites. Even John, the gourmet, found little interest in his Clamato juice and smoked oysters.

What the passage lacked in comfort, it supplied abundantly in adventure. Here was blue-water sailing's very bottom line. *Intuition* was minimal in size and equipment. Discomfort took its toll. The crew held together, however, and after twenty-one days at sea we celebrated the elation of landfall with an indulgent feast at Hilo's Pancake House. John and Jerry returned to California, ready for a safe trip to the desert. We had sampled passage making and seen the origins of a sailor's love/hate feeling for the sea and the rest of the crew. My first blue-water encounter lay astern; I wasn't at all sure what lay ahead.

Back in California, life took on a new ambiguity. Hawaii had been meant to saturate a cruising desire, but somehow it had only whetted an appetite Lenore and I attempted to sublimate by doing a bit of dinghy racing. It was truly enjoyable, but the kind of sailing we'd come to wish for did not fit in a triangular course. Tropical cruising had left a stronger impression than we had figured on.

The dilemma presented some serious problems for our family. Tara was four at this point and Eric was two. Until now our sailing had been the part-time, recreational kind. The salaries and vacation times we earned had afforded us the opportunity to do what we had done. We had stretched these factors to their limit. The cost of a larger boat and a longer cruise, in time as well as dollars, simply would not fit into the old perspective. If we were to undertake more extensive voyaging, we'd need entirely different commitments.

There were two basic options. One was to rent our house, buy an older, thirty-foot vessel to cruise in, and take a year's leave of absence from our work. This version introduced serious time and financial constraints but would allow us something to return to. Unfortunately, most thirty-foot vessels were not really suitable for a family of four on a long cruise.

The second and bolder option was to sell the house, cash in all our material possessions, and buy—or build from a kit—a larger vessel suitable for extended cruising. The concept smoldered for a long time. At first it seemed too abstract to discuss. Then one evening, at dinner, Lenore casually asked if I thought Tahiti was like Hawaii. My wife has always been a person who hated decisions but regularly made her thoughts known. We fantasized about the prospects of a voyage to Polynesia. We began to read of others who had sailed away—the Hiscocks, Roths, and Smeetons among them—and thoughts of our own cruising plans took hold. They flourished.

FINDING THE RIGHT BOAT

Intuition had given us a chance to sample blue-water cruising. She also gave us lasting insights into living aboard. We thus had good information for clarifying decisions about our prospective voyage. My cruising philosophy was a composite one, a mixture of many traditional attitudes and a preference for a modern fiberglass hull. I wanted to find a larger version of *Intuition*. The boat had to have sufficient structural integrity and the seakeeping ability necessary for passages offshore. At that point we weren't sure about the length of our voyage, but we certainly wanted a vessel that could withstand heavy weather.

Tara and Eric, here just three and a half and one and a half years old, relax aboard Wind Shadow's predecessor, Intuition. *This was a weekend sail, two years later followed by* Wind Shadow's *1,457-day voyage.*

➤ 25

Lenore and Tara look seaward at California's Santa Catalina Island—an island they would later explore on family sailing weekends.

When Lenore and I now looked seriously at boats we had a certain concept in mind. We weren't sidetracked by carved-teak cabin trim, salty-looking deadeyes, lanyards, and clipper bows. Ultralight displacement was equally unappealing. We weren't veterans, but we did have a strong notion of what we wanted.

Eventually, we discovered what we could afford. Reality narrowed our interest down to two realms: used, well-built, out-rated ocean racers and similar-sized kit boats. The latter were finally given up because a kit saved us no money if we counted our labor as a cost, and because I saw no kit hulls I particularly liked. Furthermore, quite a bit of kit boat costs were saved or lost depending on the buyer's bargain-hunting skills. Those who purchased directly from the manufacturer saved considerably. I knew of friends who made up bogus letterheads and finagled their way into astounding discounts. But I am of a weaker strain, the kind that has never walked out of a chandlery sale without buying things not on sale. My bargaining ability was poor, and I'm sure that the industry would have gone through a growth spurt if I had become involved in outfitting a forty-foot boat.

Marina del Rey is the largest boat basin in the world. Yacht brokerages surround the waterfront. Unfortunately, I didn't know that half of Los Angeles gave brokers the same story I did. As soon as greetings were exchanged, I'd let the broker know that my wife and I and our two children were planning a cruise to Polynesia. Before I could describe what I was looking for, the broker would open his "Mission Impossible" file. It usually contained a thirty-two-foot brigantine, a ferro-cement junk, and an avalanche of half-finished multihulls. On a bad day in the Catalina Channel many of these vessels would self-destruct. The prospect of an offshore passage in any of them would be more than grim.

I finally asked a brokerage associate why he was showing me such rubbish. Defensively, he blurted out, "All you daydreamers are alike, with your plans of sailing to Fiji. There's lots of talk, but you never get past Catalina." He went on to let me know that his fleet of hermaphrodites made great liveaboard vessels and that was all cruising people were interested in anyway.

I was disheartened over the events of the day and not looking forward to the long drive back to Channel Islands Harbor. Bidding farewell to the ➤ 27 smiling brokers of Marina del Rey, I abandoned the freeway system and headed for the coastal route. The surfers at Malibu seemed to be having the same luck with waves that I had had with boats. L.A. fell farther astern as I wondered if we were to become like the rest—talkers of great adventure, but never actually able to slip away. The winding coast road was a nice alternative to the freeway. Sometimes less efficiency seemed to be what I needed most.

I returned to the thought of the boat that we had yet to find—and had already named *Wind Shadow*. The first time I had heard the term "wind shadow" was when Jerry, John, and I sailed *Intuition* into Radio Bay, Hilo, Hawaii. We had tied her stern to the quay and marveled at the pleasure of going ashore. A young local sailor, Kiki by name, stopped to chat about the islands. I asked him about good areas to cruise. He mentioned a recent passage he had made around the north shore of Hawaii and Maui. The trades had been quite strong, and the passage was a wet and lumpy one. He went on to tell us how he had sailed into the "wind shadow" of Maui and discovered a different and peaceful world. Kiki's description of the experience caused the two words to linger.

A week later Lenore, Tara, Eric, and I sailed *Intuition* into the lee of Maui ourselves. One moment we were bashing along under the smallest jib and a double-reefed mainsail; the next we were almost becalmed on a flat, indigo sea. Astern, a river of waves and wind bisected our wake. It was just as Kiki had described it. Always on our voyage-to-be, after weeks at sea, we would wonder about the "wind shadow" of the next landfall. Could it be as good as what we had found in the lee of Maui?

Weeks became months and the search for the right boat intensified. It seemed that the ideal cruising boat didn't exist; and if it did we couldn't afford it. What we hoped for was a compromise—sound construction along with sailing efficiency. Was this just motherhood and apple-pie rhetoric? We finally clarified what we wanted and what we would do without.

To us the primary purpose of a cruising boat was going to sea. This did not mean that we also ascribed to a wet-bunks and a bucket-for-a-head version of masochism. *Intuition* had been a little too close to the water and deficit in amenities for an enjoyable passage. We needed good-quality, fundamental equipment such as storm sails and good ground tackle. Com-

fortable, dry sea berths, a well-positioned navigator's table, and a gim-baled, properly installed stove with an oven were also essential. Seemingly minor issues such as good ventilation, well-made pumps, and a self-steering system that really works are major concerns at sea. Certain fiberglass production boats, built in the mid-sixties, seemed to fit our needs. Their solid glass hull laminates are as thick as a plank. In a gale in the lonely reaches of the Pacific, an overbuilt hull is comforting indeed.

The Ericson 41 was designed by Bruce King in 1966. Its traditional shear and profile were blended into an underbody incorporating an elongated fin keel and separate rudder. A combination of low wetted surface, moderate weight, and a good-sized sail plan afforded excellent light-air performance. The 47 percent ballast ratio, six feet of draft, and ten-foot eight-inch beam added the righting characteristics desirable in an offshore passage maker. The advent of the IOR rule relegated many healthy CCA designs to Wednesday night club races.

"The Ericson 41 was one of them," said the broker sitting across from me. We were discussing hull #23; a sloop named *Alura*. I knew I was in trouble at first glance. The broker recognized the "this-is-the-one" look on my face. I'm not much of a negotiator, as I've said, and couldn't get rid of the "this-is-it-at-any-price" feeling growing within me. The double-spreader rig, low-profile cabin trunk, and clean white hull were right. The broker knew he had me.

With confidence, the broker now mentioned that the owner's daughter would be here shortly and we could get a look at the well-appointed varnished-mahogany interior. The brochure he showed me revealed the functional layout. The hook sank deeper.

Before long the daughter arrived and the combination lock opened. With an air of self-assurance, the broker thrust the hatch forward, ready to land his fish. He cringed, staggered, and almost fainted as the odor of ninety-five-degree cabin air, scented with the aroma of a broken holding tank, reached his nostrils. The carpets had been awash and the bilges didn't meet the EPA standards. The negotiating advantage was broken.

I raced back to Channel Islands Harbor to bring Lenore the good news. I described the boat, her rig and sailing potential. We talked about the U-shaped galley and the chart table to starboard. Finally, I mentioned ➤ 29 the cabin catastrophe. It was hard to convince Lenore that it still might be a good alternative. A day later I convinced her at least to have a look for herself.

We returned to *Alura*. Despite the Clorox rinse and a half-dozen Airwicks, the outhouse ambience lingered. Lenore's reluctance to get involved shook the already wavering price. To make a long story short, we decided that *Alura* was definitely it. I was sure that the present problems could be completely rectified. (They were.) We worked out an attractive agreement and, thereafter, have always felt that it was the best ("shitty") luck we have ever had.

Halfway Between House and Boat

Perhaps the most trying moments were the ones when we were halfway between the house and the boat. Lenore was preparing the house and showing it to prospective buyers. I was in Marina del Rey installing a teak cabin sole aboard the recently fumigated and renamed sloop *Wind Shadow*. We were surrounded by deadlines and financial constraints.

It is hard to forget the day we sold our home. I had been up most of the night before, fastening and gluing strips of teak into place for the sole. The next morning I was scheduled to drive back home and fix a minor plumbing leak before the potential buyer arrived. All seemed to be proceeding on time, at least until I tackled the dripping faucet. My effort to tighten the fitting made a pipe burst inside the wall. A horizontal geyser soaked the washroom and all its contents. The deluge continued for several dreadful minutes until I could get to the main water-shutoff valve. Feverishly we bailed out the house. Lenore reminded me that the buyer was due in fifteen minutes. Fortunately, he didn't ask to use the bathroom. The papers were signed and we were one step closer to sailing away. Since then, I have always carried tapered bung plugs just in case someday I do the same thing to a through-hull fitting.

The next phase of our transitional life involved parting with years of material accumulations. Garage sales were as much a part of California as Disneyland and at times they were equally entertaining. We sold furniture, stereo equipment, clothes, tools, surfboards, and an array of other valuable and worthless items.

It is uncomfortable to be confronted with your own shortcomings. For years Lenore had accused me of being a junk collector, incapable of parting with things I would never use. I had known she was wrong. The truth surfaced as I emptied the attic. Broken radios, dismantled outboard motors, and box after box of useless scraps reappeared.

At first my ego necessitated putting price tags on the treasures. Before long the signs were changed to half-price, then, finally, to FREE. A few seasoned garage-sale veterans looked at the items and left with a smile, some offering unappreciated comments.

At last I was vindicated. A middle-aged fellow eagerly gathered up the boxes with statements such as ". . . just what I've been looking for." I couldn't leave well enough alone. I had to ask the chap what he was going to use such an esoteric collection for. His answer was painfully clarifying. He was doing concrete work and needed junk to use for fill. Costly cement would be saved. Lenore offered a wistful smile. I wasn't totally cured, but I was 95 percent improved. As time went on, there was only one locker aboard *Wind Shadow* that seemed to gather what might be termed "poorly placed" ballast. It was regularly attended to, and most of the truly useless items went ashore or overboard. If nothing else, cruising streamlined my material priorities.

Our transition from shore life to life aboard a cruising boat was quite complex, to put it mildly. We spent a year adjusting to the change. During this period *Wind Shadow* was berthed in a local marina. Tara was now a ladylike five and Eric an energized three. Our daily routine stayed much the same as it had been ashore. On weekends we'd disconnect the power cord and docklines and sail to our favorite Santa Barbara Channel Islands. The mini-cruises gave us a chance to check out recently added gear and cruising concepts. I can't emphasize enough how important these field tests were for us. The time to discover a self-steering gear problem is when it is first installed, not when you're five days out on a passage to an island two thousand miles away. And living aboard in such a controlled environment gave all four of us the chance to adjust to our new surroundings.

➤ 31

Perhaps it is a mistake to begin something you're not absolutely sure about. If so, it is not surprising that at this point Lenore and I had some serious misgivings about our cruising plans. Anxiety and indecision began to tinge our daydreams. Our thoughts had dwelled upon the pleasures of South Seas landfalls, but it wasn't long before some pitfalls also became apparent. Rumors of uninsured vessels being pulverized on surf-swept reefs, the thought of someone falling overboard, and the dangers imposed by an unpredictable hurricane season—all of these challenged our grand fantasies. Fortunately, we survived the initial "what-if" crisis.

Uncertainty may have even prompted better preparation. Lenore and I weren't escapists. Nor were we part of the daydream fleet that sailed away unprepared, hoping to learn navigation on the way to Tahiti. Lenore was a teacher and I was an assistant principal of a junior high school. We had been entrenched in suburbia. We had children, PTA membership cards, and a charge account at Sears. Getting ready for an extended cruise was therefore one of the most complex aspects of the entire voyage.

Our biggest hurdle, however, was a philosophical one. We had little trouble deciding that extended cruising was the right option for Lenore and me, but it was hard to make the same commitment for our children. Well-meaning friends reminded us of what Tara and Eric would be missing. They told us the disadvantages of transiency and of the absence of a "normal school experience." We pondered all these things.

Looking back at our worries and complex preparations before departure, I am amazed that *Wind Shadow* ever set sail. But somehow we severed our ties, got everything ready, and began a voyage headed west.

We departed with an abundance of apprehensions, and five years and a thousand unforgettable experiences later *Wind Shadow*'s wake had stretched across three oceans. Tara and Eric were educated underway and thrived, despite dire forewarnings of "cultural starvation." We answered some questions and discovered new uncertainties. One thing we were sure of: if sailing away had been a mistake, it was the most fortunate mistake of our lives.

Provisioning for Wind Shadow's *lengthy voyage included food for Bosley the cat and, with Eric's assistance, Dinty Moore for the crew.*

With the decision made and provisioning nearly complete, Wind Shadow *heads past Channel Islands Harbor breakwater on an afternoon's sail (photograph by Ed Matisoff).*

CHAPTER 2

First Passage—Hawaii and the Pacific

On June 26, 1976, *Wind Shadow* set sail from Channel Islands Harbor, California. At first it seemed as if we were headed for another weekend rendezvous with the familiar roly anchorages of Santa Cruz Island. But as the jagged island peaks faded astern, we realized the significance of our departure. Ahead of us lay Hawaii and beyond. Behind us lay burned bridges, impossible to rebuild. In less than a year we had transformed a very dependent shoreside life-style into one of mobility and independence. One lingering question remained. Would the new way of life be worth the sacrifices involved?

The answer was to unfold gradually. We realized that the first passage would set certain parameters of what was to follow. I had given considerable thought to my previous voyage to Hawaii aboard *Intuition*. I recalled the despair of departure. Friends and relatives had given Jerry, John, and me a dockside farewell. It was too emotional a way to start a cruise. This time Lenore and I had shared good-byes with friends beforehand. When *Wind Shadow* was finally fully provisioned, fueled, and ready to go we quietly slipped away. Hawaii was a familiar destination. My family was aboard and this kind of departure seemed more fitting.

We were prepared for the less-than-ideal conditions of the first few days of a passage. Most likely they would include a predominance of gray, sullen overcast. The wind would be forward of the beam and stronger than we would prefer. It would take several days for our sea legs to develop, and *mal de mer* could make the prospect of a 2,300-mile voyage seem bleak. As it turned out, the weather was about what I had anticipated, but only the skipper had some difficulty in stabilizing his sea legs. Tara and Eric played with toys in the well-padded confines of the dinette converted into a double berth and enclosed by a substantial leeboard. During the day they often joined us in the cockpit. From the beginning we familiarized Tara and Eric with as much of *Wind Shadow's* workings as they were able to cope with.

Children acclimate to sailing rather easily, we found. They are inquisitive and, if allowed to participate, their competencies can be staggering. There were three phases to our involvement of Tara and Eric in the new life we planned to share. The first stressed swimming and water safety. Besides being important as a "stay-afloat" issue, it helped attune our children to the pleasures found in and around the sea. Watching them react to the warm, clear water of Hawaii during that first summer would give us some hint of the potential for the coming years.

We encouraged Tara and Eric to explore the waters surrounding them. At first their adventures were quite controlled. We paddled rubber rafts together, leaning over the side and peering into the shallow depths with face masks. They had found it hard to learn to use a snorkel and a mask together, so we showed them how to use the dive mask first and later added the snorkel. A life jacket and a dive mask became their favorite summer toys.

Lenore and I also encouraged their use of the dinghy. The seven-foot fiberglass pram became another toy, and rowing skills were the first fringe benefit. Life jackets were mandatory during these early episodes of boat handling.

Our children had first begun to row in the confines of the Channel Islands Harbor Marina. Initially they had had difficulties coordinating their strokes, but eventually even feathering their oars between strokes came naturally. We had also taught Tara and Eric how to make a painter fast to a cleat and how to tie a bowline. These were not hard-core training sessions for future contenders for collegiate rowing awards; they were simple efforts that involved our children in the water-oriented life we aspired to. The sessions seemed to work. At four and six Tara and Eric could row their dinghy along the rocky bulkhead near our slip, observing sea stars, sculpins, and an occasional octopus. If they enjoyed the fauna of D dock, imagine what a Polynesian lagoon had in store for them.

I had then added a sailing rig to the dinghy, renamed it *Taric,* and further expanded the scope of the children's adventures. Without Top-Siders or a working knowledge of a yachting vocabulary, they learned to sail. At first Lenore or I would sail the dinghy with either Tara or Eric. Sheet handling and steering finally developed into the kids taking mom and dad for a sail. Watching them single-hand was another of the steps on the way to sharing a family commitment. I felt encouraged by their accomplishments.

Throughout these learning experiences in California, Lenore and I tried to maintain a low-key, safety-first outlook. Whether swimming or sailing, we kept Tara and Eric under close but unobtrusive supervision. We generally let them remedy their own mistakes. When a serious error was made, which might evolve into a real problem, we came to the rescue. Once, for instance, Tara and Eric got caught downwind in *Taric.* Then when it was time to come back the wind was too strong. We went after them with another dinghy, and from that experience they learned the deceptions in sailing downwind.

It is important, we realized, that parents expose their children to such learning-through-doing encounters but maintain control of the situation. We were constantly aware of the effects of wind and current. We knew the characteristics of the dinghy—how much positive floatation it had, the best way to right it after a capsize. Once a child develops a fear of the water, it is a difficult memory to erase.

The next phase of our tutorial approach to cruising took place aboard *Wind Shadow* once we were under way. Tara and Eric were an active part of the crew from the very beginning. At first their tricks at the helm were unscheduled and ad-libbed. On light-wind days they helped us with headsail changes. Their expertise at bagging the drifter grew each time they handled it. They ran sheets through blocks, learned to crank winches, and practiced the omnipotent bowline. Seamanship lessons were kept short, varied, and attuned to their grasshopper attention spans. Bit by bit the way *Wind Shadow* worked became apparent to them.

The third phase of our effort to inculcate Tara and Eric with a love of the sea was perhaps the most important. Ironically, it was also the least organized. It began ashore and came aboard with us. Boats, ocean science, and interest in islands naturally dominated our family conversa- ➤ 37 tions. Our children soon became familiar with the context and joined in the dialogue. Hull shapes and sail plans began appearing in Eric's artwork. His sister preferred seascapes of islands, seabirds, and sunsets. Both talked of changing *Taric* from a leeboard dinghy to a centerboarder. Close quarters helped to further the concept of a family commitment. It was rewarding to watch our children make the transition from passenger status to crew status.

We discovered on this first passage too that the larger vessel made a world of difference to our whole family. *Wind Shadow's* behavior was more subdued than *Intuition's* had been; she simply took average offshore conditions in stride. Self-steering gear relieved the tedium of helm responsibility and made watchkeeping for a shorthanded crew more endurable. The cabin remained dry, the galley was usable at sea, and the crew had their own comfortable berths. What had been an ordeal on the earlier passage became easily tolerable now.

For five days we headed south from Channel Islands Harbor until the cold, damp westerlies finally subsided. During my fifth night watch the stars returned to the sky and a hint of a northeasterly began to fill in. The next morning brought a trade wind reunion. Suddenly the sun was shining, hatches were open, and we were flying over a flat sea with a consistent 15-knot breeze. The sheets were eased and *Wind Shadow* could now head west toward Hawaii.

The days that followed unfolded as they should. Porpoises came to swim through our bow waves. Flying fish skimmed across the wave crests and long-tailed tropic birds reminded us that this was cruising at its best. We all felt exhilarated.

Wind Shadow's cutter-rig modification was working out well. It allowed the sail area in the foretriangle to be handled with ease. I could drop one of the two headsails to compensate for increased wind velocity; if it was a squall of minor concern I usually doused the forestaysail. This cut the sail area in the foretriangle nearly in half and was a simple procedure. Without changing course or even easing the sheet, I could slip the halyard and allow the sail to fall to the deck inside the slot created by the Yankee jib topsail and the mainsail. Conventional piston hanks held the luff securely

Vital friend to Wind Shadow's *shorthanded crew was this* Aries *self-steering gear, which could handle varying wind, sea, and point-of-sail requirements.*

➤ 39

In trade wind calms Tara and Eric enjoyed the foredeck, for daydreams and gazing. Bosley found time to search for misguided flying fish.

to the inner forestay, and all I had to do was tie two gaskets to bunch the sail along the leeward rail. When the breeze subsided we simply hauled up the forestaysail again.

Normally I carried a single reef in the mainsail when the breeze was strong enough to call for the double-headsail rig I've been mentioning. Most trade wind sailing is just that: 15 knots of breeze or better. When it comes time to change to a larger or smaller sail, one headsail stays set during the sail change. The vessel keeps moving and retains some balance in her sail plan, which is appreciated by both the crew and the self-steering gear.

Running backstays didn't seem to be the nuisance that we'd been told they would be. To the contrary, there is something reassuring about their added support. Another fringe benefit is the handhold they provide for the crew headed from cockpit to foredeck. *Wind Shadow*'s sail plan and rig turned out to be very easy for our family to handle.

Warm, sunny days were what we had been looking for on our first leg. The June/July passage to Hawaii meant we would sail directly under the midday zenith sun. At one point its declination and our latitude would be identical. It wasn't long before we had forgotten about the chill of the westerlies.

Wind Shadow's cockpit well now became a wading pool for Tara and Eric. In the afternoons we plugged the scuppers and poured seawater into the confines. Our children played with toy boats in their seagoing bathtub.

At one point I used their game to explain how a current can set a vessel off course. Eric was pushing his plastic tugboat athwartships from port to starboard. Both he and Tara could see that the toy boat traveled a certain measurable distance. But *Wind Shadow* herself was definitely moving in a different direction and carrying the toy boat with her. So Eric's tug had been moving in at least two different directions at once. Just like a toy boat in a cockpit bathtub, *Wind Shadow* was in an ocean basin of water that was moving in a direction different from her own course. At that point the current happened to be helping us toward Hawaii. "Imagine if the current were moving the *opposite* way and our knotmeter read six knots? How fast would we really be going?" I asked. After some pensive moments, Tara responded with, "Not fast enough, Dad."

➤ 41

* * *

In all, *Wind Shadow's* shakedown cruise went well. Only one major problem had presented itself and, naturally, it had to be a mechanical one. I must admit that I had been intimidated by the engine room. The diesel had been serviced prior to departure and I convinced myself that there would be plenty of time to learn about its idiosyncracies at some later point. I didn't realize how right I was. Unfortunately, I also didn't realize that Murphy schedules when and where these mechanical interludes take place.

Inexcusable chauvinistic male ego had convinced me of my mechanical aptitude. At age twelve I began taking apart and putting back together, more or less, my 2½-horsepower Johnson Seahorse outboard motor. By age eighteen I knew how to adjust the points on my 1954 Plymouth and understood why filing the intake and exhaust ports of a 50-horsepower Mercury outboard motor would make it go faster. Unfortunately, none of these esoteric skills seemed applicable to the diesel hidden beneath *Wind Shadow's* companionway ladder. Perhaps it was the halo of hoses and wires that intimidated me most. Whatever the reason, I avoided precruise familiarity with troubleshooting techniques. I had at least put aboard two toolboxes.

My first battle with the engine took place halfway to Hawaii on one of those classical trade wind days. *Wind Shadow* was sleigh-riding down cresting seas. Surfing a ten-ton vessel is exhilarating. I decided to start the engine and run it for an hour to charge the batteries. Lenore switched on the power for starting and I turned the ignition key. The starter made a dull clunk and then there was silence. I assumed that the starting battery was low, so asked Lenore to switch to the BOTH battery position. A second attempt had the same outcome. I could see that a new ritual was about to begin.

Lenore relieved me at the helm and I went below to resolve the problem. The large trade wind seas enhanced the ambience of sticking my head into the confines of the bilge. My analytical mind was feeling a bit woozy.

I checked the voltage in each battery and saw that there was plenty of starting current available. Next I removed the starter and tested it. I was sure it was the problem. It wasn't. The starter was replaced, and I went

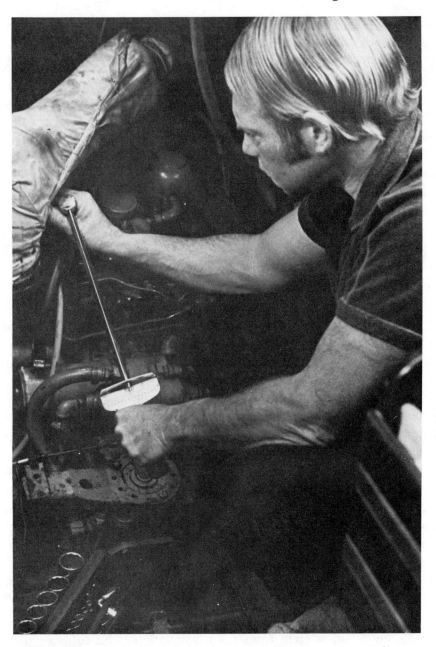

*Wind Shadow's errant 37-hp diesel was a stranger to the author at first, but, of
necessity, not for long.*

➤ 43

topside to gasp some clean air and momentarily hang over the rail. Eric told his sister that Dad was saying nasty things to the engine again.

Undaunted and recovered, I returned to my bane. By this time I was really confused. Obviously, something was preventing the engine from turning over. Could a piece of the starter ring gear be broken off and wedged against the housing? I discovered that a 1⅛-inch socket fit the crankshaft pulley nut. Affixing the socket to a breaker bar, I tried to turn the engine over manually. It barely budged. I could move it only a small amount in each direction.

The afternoon light was waning. The motion and confines below kept me feeling green, and I contemplated removing the engine head to see if something had broken off and wedged itself in a cylinder. I disconnected the injector tubing and began to pull the injectors. The first tip seemed to be wet. Once I had all four out, I gave the breaker bar a yank and earned a faceful of seawater.

It took me a while to figure out how I had ended up with such a hydraulic-lock problem. I had plenty of time to think about it as I bailed out each cylinder. A small syringe from our medical kit and a bit of small-diameter hose facilitated the process. After the water was extracted, I refilled each cylinder with alcohol to act as a dessicant against residual water. Next I refilled each cylinder with diesel fuel.

After pumping out the residue for the third time, I decided to crank the engine over before I put the injectors back in. I pushed the starter button and felt as if I had dropped the forty-five-pound CQR anchor on my foot. The breaker bar, which had been attached to the crankshaft pulley, had just spun around and landed squarely on my instep. Fortunately, nothing was broken. I verbalized my concern. Eric told his mother that the engine must really be in bad shape.

An hour later I had the beast reassembled and the oil changed, just in case any water had gotten past the rings, and had limped back up on deck. The engine started. Tara and Eric were impressed by the performance. Lenore wondered what was wrong with my foot.

It is obviously worthwhile to do some engine homework before a cruise. Many troubles stem from poor installation. The cylinder trauma just mentioned was caused by an inadequately designed exhaust system. When *Wind Shadow* heeled in a seaway and was moving near hull speed, water was siphoned back through the exhaust system into the cylinders via the exhaust manifold. After that, whenever I shut the engine down I removed the exhaust hose at the through-hull fitting and put a bung plug in the hole. I added a shut-off valve in Hawaii and, eventually, a new exhaust system in New Zealand.

It was the nights on that first leg that made us aware of our true detachment from land. The isolation of night watches gave us time to ponder. I'd stand much of the night watch on my own, spelled by Lenore as need be. She'd take over just after dawn. At first we all found the lack of good vision at night disconcerting. But night vision improved, thanks to the adaptability of the human eye; the retina must be the envy of Kodak's filmmakers. We found reflected starlight to be illumination enough to defeat complete darkness. When the moon was full there seemed to be twenty-four hours of daylight. We became so accustomed to the low light level of a night watch that we had to put a resister in line with the compass light to dull its overly bright red glow. During daylight hours we couldn't tell whether the binnacle light was on or off. The latitude of the human visual response is astounding.

Spreader lights were fine for helping dinner guests into a tender while in port. At sea they were too bright. They destroyed night vision and did more to hinder a sail change than help it. Refracted light from the mid-mast bow light was more than enough illumination on the foredeck. I finally moved one of *Wind Shadow's* spreader lights around to the top of the spreader to illuminate the upper part of the sail. It became an anti-collision device, lit to reveal our location to vessels nearby.

A tricolor masthead light proved to be an efficient running-light alternative. On several occasions I made contact with the merchant ships via VHF Channel 16. I asked the officer on the bridge about the visibility of *Wind Shadow's* running lights. A switch below allowed me to change from the tricolor masthead light to the conventional hull-mounted sidelights. The masthead version received unanimous approval, while the sidelights sometimes couldn't even be seen. I was also informed that *Wind Shadow* left a good image on the radar screen. I'm not sure whether that was due to the reflector I used or to the spar itself, but it was reassuring.

Night watches in trade wind regions were a pleasure to keep. Most ➤ 45 steering obligations were handled by our silent partner, the Aries pendulum servo vane gear. Lenore and I often disengaged it, though, and steered for the sheer pleasure of being at the helm of a trade wind passage maker. We regularly maintained a deck watch, even in regions where there was little chance of crossing wakes with anything other than flying fish and friendly porpoises. In these isolated ocean areas, watchkeeping became less diligent.

Trade wind squalls are not a friend of the passage maker. They are unpredictable and can send spars and torn sails right over the side. On clear nights we could usually see them coming early enough for reefing and sail changes. Overcast, moonless conditions, however, were sometimes a problem. And the frequency of heavy squalls increases in very humid trade wind weather.

I recall one episode quite vividly. I was on deck during a night passage and *Wind Shadow* was moving efficiently through a flat sea. The breeze had increased to about 18 knots. We carried one reef in the main, the inner forestaysail, and the small Yankee jib. The sky was completely overcast and several weak squalls had meekly passed over. All they had demanded was a reduction in headsail area; I doused the Yankee jib topsail and ran off before the puffs under main and staysail. The technique worked well.

Squall number three was a totally different story. The first gust made it clear that this was going to be the real thing. I headed off so the wind was on the starboard quarter. *Wind Shadow* began to leap through the water. Lenore scrambled on deck and took the helm, while I raced forward to get the staysail down and try to get another reef in the main. The staysail cooperated and I soon had it lashed securely to the rail. But the main sheet had been eased to avoid rounding up under the impact of the stronger gusts, and now the main was pinned to the spreaders and the leeward shrouds.

Wind Shadow's steering characteristics were poor under mainsail alone. I decided to set the staysail again and run off with the more balanced sail plan. The main was also immobilized by a boom vang and a preventer that ran forward to the bow. If we broached, there would be a true fire drill.

The sea was relatively smooth, however, and it was a good opportunity to see what our sloop's steering characteristics were like under such conditions. The knotmeter was regularly reading 10 knots. The rig hummed and the hull vibrated with each increasing gust. The forestaysail did its job well. As we were forced up to windward with each overpowering gust, the staysail kept the bow from rounding up. *Wind Shadow* remained responsive to the helm. She flew before the squall at speeds we could hardly have imagined. The windward running backstay quivered and all I could think of was what would happen if the spar let go. But the squall finally subsided, and we had a chance to regain our composure. I felt exhausted. Tara and Eric slept through the whole episode!

Larger seas would, of course, have changed the picture drastically. I would have had to get the mainsail down or at least more deeply reefed. We'd have had to head up enough to free the sail from the shrouds and spreaders. The gusty conditions would surely have ripped the sail.

In the squalls I realized a few things that had long-lasting significance for us. First of all, the shorthanded crew has no business being caught in such a circumstance when an alternative exists, which, of course, it had for us. There is too much chance of gear failure or a crew mistake leading to catastrophe. If one of us had gone overboard, *Wind Shadow* would have sailed half a mile downwind before vang and preventer could be released and the vessel turned into the wind. Even so, it would have been impossible to power to windward in such conditions. Aside from this, nothing could be heard above the scream of the wind. A person overboard in these conditions could easily be lost. We should instead have dropped the main early and proceeded under forestaysail alone. This tactic later proved its worth to us again and again, especially in Australia and Africa, where squalls are even more infamous.

We also learned something about lightning on this first passage. Worry over being struck is an absolutely valid concern. On one occasion our isolated backstay—serving also as a radio antenna—glowed with a blue covering of Saint Elmo's fire. We also saw lightning hit the water several miles from us. Apparently, *Wind Shadow* has a properly bonded and grounded hull and rig or we have been very lucky; perhaps a little of each.

The crew of the forty-foot-sloop *Dragon* weren't as fortunate as we ➤ 47 were. A few months later, while anchored in the San Blas Islands off the coast of Central America, they were directly hit by lightning. Surprisingly, *Dragon's* rig is not as tall as several others that were in the anchorage or as tall as the trees on a nearby hillside. The strike resulted in massive damage to electrical equipment, a burn to skipper Lou Czukelter's finger, and *Dragon's* near sinking. A through-hull fitting was blown out of the hull in the same manner as an overloaded capacitor can explode in a TV set. Quick action on the part of the crew resulted in the hole being plugged and the vessel being saved.

I'm not sure what the actual chances are of a boat being hit by lightning. I do believe that installing a bonded electrical system and a good grounded mast connection will eliminate some of the hazard. It will also add some psychological security.

HAWAII AT LAST

After seventeen days at sea, our first passage neared its end as we sighted the Big Island of Hawaii. Tara and Eric were tired of splashing in the cockpit well and were eager to return to the beaches they had enjoyed two years before. I was surprised at how different *Wind Shadow's* passage had been from my earlier crossing in *Intuition*. That passage had been more of an adventurous ordeal—the smaller vessel exaggerated the effects of wind and sea. *Wind Shadow* took the same offshore conditions right in stride. Our passage was drier, safer, and more enjoyable. In fact, Lenore was surprised at how well our whole family had adapted to confinement and isolation. The lack of TV and playgrounds hadn't really fazed Tara and Eric at all, and we only occasionally missed things like ice cream and cold drinks.

Fine things had happened to us all. We had watched the seabirds soar in the trade winds and seen whales gliding through the sea. The routine that developed aboard *Wind Shadow* seemed to follow a similar rhythm. When the breeze was light and the day clear, we sunbathed, read, and exercised on deck. In lots of wind we just held on tight and frowned occasionally. We swam when we were absolutely becalmed—only once on the way to Hawaii, more often on other passages. Tara and Eric

With Wind Shadow *becalmed a thousand miles from land, her crew had a chance for a swim and some thoughts about an ocean three miles deep.*

turned the cabin into a stage for the adventures of King Arthur. What they lacked in room they made up for in fantasy.

Swimming in water three miles deep and a thousand miles from the nearest beach, incidentally, is a bit disconcerting. Either Lenore or I stayed on deck, playing lifeguard and standing shark watch while the other swam with the children, next to the boat. One might consider such a diversion foolhardy. What would happen if the wind came up suddenly or if a strange current moved us away from the vessel? Well, life is filled with chances. The parent who decides that a child is skilled enough and old enough to ride a bicycle to the store makes a value judgment; there are cars on the road and an accident could be lethal. Swimming at sea really isn't any different from swimming near shore. We trailed a safety line astern and always stayed close to the ladder. If the swimmers are competent and the proper conditions are chosen, it's probably safer than riding a bicycle to the store.

We all learned some things about food and refrigeration, too. Once the last chunk of our three hundred pounds of ice had melted, our suburban diet and refrigerator cuisine came to a halt. Our concept of the "only drink being a cold drink" perished. Lukewarm grapefruit Tang wasn't welcomed with enthusiasm, but fortunately I had installed a good charcoal filter, and the water from *Wind Shadow*'s tank was quite palatable. Bit by bit we discovered that ice wasn't quite as important as oxygen and there could be life even without refrigeration.

Lenore saved the day with her treats from the oven. Nearly every day Tara, Eric, and I had the chance to judge her Chocolate Crazy cake and delectable pies and fresh whole wheat bread—superior to Betty Crocker's finest. These fresh-baked delights offset our "no-ice" despondency. It was fortunate that we had replaced a poorly constructed alcohol stove with a stainless-steel Shipmate propane unit. I realized the hazard associated with the heavier-than-air gas, and installed the tanks out on deck and put a safety shut-off where the fuel entered the cabin.

We arrived in Hilo, Hawaii, fit, a few pounds lighter, and glad once again to step ashore. The passage had been a luxury cruise when compared to the Spartan life aboard *Intuition*.

The volcanic peaks of the Hawaiian Islands are hard to forget. Our first sight of them misrepresented their magnitude. For an entire day they

As the journey's first leg nears completion, Hawaii is at last in sight and Wind Shadow's bow lookouts can relax.

grew in size as we approached the island. It wasn't until 0200 the following day that *Wind Shadow* finally reached Hilo.

The island chain is a display of rugged volcanism offset by soft trade wind clouds. When whaling ships sailed into the lee of Maui, the sea and the mountains must have looked just the same as they do now. Ashore it is a different story. Hawaii is a cornerstone of Polynesia. It is also an extension of Los Angeles. Tourists, escaping the confines of their suburban life, shop in the Ali Wai Mall, paddle about in traditional fiberglass outriggers, and listen to the melodies of Don Ho and his electric band. The cruising sailor interested in finding the old ways of Polynesia is relegated to the Bishop Museum or a voyage to the south, away from the jet routes and travel agent intrusion.

There is nevertheless a lot to experience in Hawaii. In 1974 we had sailed *Intuition* into the Ali Wai Yacht Harbor. The Hawaii Yacht Club made us feel at home. Eric Metcalf, as port captain, seemed to do all he could for visiting transients. He too had sailed to Hawaii. At the H.Y.C. Eric arranged guest slips and hot showers. If something needed fixing he knew where to go and how to get there. Much of the time it turned out that Eric would give you a ride on his own time after work. Again in 1976 we stopped at the club and found the same warm hospitality. Eric was still there, and still enthusiastic about the fleet of cruising vessels that indulge in the club's offer of showers and civilized dining.

A year later we met Eric in Tahiti aboard his sloop *Kohikimoe*. He too had found some time to pursue his cruising interest and was en route to the Austral Islands. The last I heard from the skipper of *Kohikimoe* he was headed back to Hawaii. Perhaps we will cross wakes again.

The name of the native Hawaiian we met at Manelle Bay, Lanai, is lost to us, but we well remember him. Our friendship began with an idle chat about our home port and sailing experiences, about how the children had fared on the seventeen-day passage. He soon asked if we'd like to see a bit of his island. During the next three hours he drove us up a pine-clad mountain slope to the refreshing coolness of Lanai City. The tales he told us ranged from how the Dole pineapple-harvesting facility worked to what went on in the islands during World War II. The afternoon had been glorious. Back at the boat I offered our friend some reimbursement

Vessels Wind Shadow *and* Silky *lie at anchor in the lee of Kaui, Hawaii, eighty-four days out of Channel Islands Harbor.*

for all the fuel he had used. He refused to take it. "Aloha," the Hawaiian word for welcome, took on a new meaning for us.

Before heading on we visited Hanalei Bay, a sailor's refuge during the trade wind months of summer. A white, crescent-shaped shoreline lies at the foot of one of the wettest mountains in the world. An amazing 360 inches of rain each year feed the waterfalls of Hanalei Valley. From our anchorage we could see ribbons of white water falling from the green slopes. The sea is clear, and we found waves to surf and reefs aplenty to explore. Friends met earlier in the islands—John and Irmgard Conley and Bob and Betty Sisler—were anchored near us aboard their vessels *Cara* and *Kalona*. There in Hanalei Bay daydreams of sailing on to French Polynesia were recounted and plans made. The next anchorage we would share with *Cara* and her crew would be nestled inside the Bora Bora Lagoon.

FANNING ISLAND AND TONGAREVA

Fanning Island is a lost speck in an out-of-the-way portion of the Pacific. It lies almost midway between Hawaii and French Polynesia, and is the antithesis of Hawaii's Oahu. The low coral atoll's tallest peak rises only about twelve feet above sea level.

Our approach to the island was inadvertently well timed. The clear tropical water affords the best visibility when the sun is overhead. Seeing what you are sailing over can be a distinct advantage.

The pass into the inner lagoon is the prototype of threading cautiously through the jaws of a coral reef. Surf bursts on each side of the pass and aids to navigation are not of a man-made variety. Polaroid sunglasses and steps on the mast, leading aloft to the spreaders, were worth their weight in gold to me that day.

By the time I reached *Wind Shadow*'s first set of crosstrees, it seemed as if the water was gone and our sloop floated eerily above the coral. I called to Tara to read the depth sounder. What looked like seven feet was really forty. The visual appearance was unnerving. We were entering on a flood tide of 5 knots. Our speed over the ground—and thus the enhanced danger in running aground—was staggering.

We made it. Once through the pass we tucked into the lee of the anchorage, breathed a sigh of relief, and succumbed to the sound of natives singing, palms rustling, and the reality of traditional Polynesia.

We spent some fascinating days at Fanning Island with much exploring and talking. Once every six months a Banks Line freighter stops by to load coconuts and deliver luxuries such as flour, rice, sugar, and woven cotton cloth. Four hundred Gilbertese and Ellice Islanders inhabit the island and work for the Burns Philip Company. Their life is simple and closely linked to traditional Polynesian ways. Western religion has infiltrated their life-style, though there still seems to be more singing than praying.

Bill Frew, whom one of the islanders invited us to meet soon after our arrival, is the only Anglo on the island. He is originally from Australia and has found that his life on Fanning Island more than makes up for what he left behind. As manager of the island's copra-harvesting operation he leads a benevolent dictator's role, in a kind of system that exists almost nowhere else in the world. Bill administers the working as well as the living aspects of the tiny island community.

At the time we visited Fanning Island, Bill was attempting to discover who was behind what we came to call "the coconut still." Some of the islanders were engaged in ingeniously fermenting the sap of the coconut palm. Apparently the clandestine activity led to a decrease in copra productivity and dissension among residents. I'm not sure what Bill decided to do about the problem, but it does seem that human dynamics are consistent regardless of whether one speaks of Fanning Island or Bayonne, New Jersey.

Copra is pretty interesting stuff, we learned from several of the islanders. It is the by-product of harvesting coconuts. Mature nuts are gathered or picked from the trees, split open, and dried on special sheltered drying racks. One specific variety of crab has adapted itself to eating these coconuts and is a definite competitor to the harvesting operation. Another species stalks every other type of vegetation on the island. Gardens must be screened in and elevated to be safe.

I also met a boatbuilder on Fanning Island who builds canoes as his ancestors did a thousand years before. Another Fanning Islander knew of our interest and asked if we'd like to go see the vessels. The builder's outrigger canoes were powered by sails woven from pandanus reed. The main hull and the *áma* (outrigger) were lashed together, using string made from the fibrous husk of a coconut. The dimensions of the vessel were based upon the span of a human hand. All measurements were multiples of a hand's width. A small man with a small hand ended up with a smaller boat. It seemed quite logical.

Our explorations yielded much other interesting information. A few of these Gilbertese Islanders still sailed in the traditional manner. Their voyages were made without compass, sextant, or chart. They utilized the same landfall-finding cues as their ancestors—apparently the sidereal setting and rising points of celestial bodies. The flight habits of seabirds and a kinesthetic awareness of currents and swells were components of their navigational system.

The great voyages by Polynesians are no longer being made. In outposts like Fanning Island, however, traces of the seafaring tradition remain alive. Eventually Western technology will arrive, but for now it was as if we had stepped back several hundred years in time. We were surprised at first to discover that life could go on without what we had grown to assume were basics; technically, life was simple. But behaviorally, Fanning Islanders have as complex a social structure as any Western civilization might have. Their approach toward life is streamlined by fewer alternatives. At present the status quo is reflected in the smiles of the inhabitants. Both disposition and dental conditions attest to some advantages of their isolation. The average wage was about one dollar a day. The people were healthy and happy. Lenore and I reevaluated our definitions of poverty.

The scientific community has renamed the Doldrums. Today they are referred to as the Intertropical Convergence Zone, or ITCZ for short. *Wind Shadow*'s passage south from Fanning Island carried us across the equator and through the belt of calms, cursed by many early sailors. It was a strange voyage, quite out of context with what we expected.

The northeast trade winds gradually dissipated, and the searing equatorial heat inspired us to fabricate a variety of awnings and wind scoops. *Wind Shadow* now began to look like a Conestoga wagon. She rolled and slatted in the midday calms. I cranked over the iron genoa and pointed the bow toward the Southern Hemisphere.

At first the autopilot was on its best behavior and handled the job of steering politely. Unfortunately, the heat must have broiled some diodes, however, for erratic responses began to surface. A friend had called his self-steering gear "cowboy" for this very behavior. It liked to "round up."

Despite the reluctance of the autopilot we crossed the equator, entered the Southern Hemisphere, and discovered what the ITCZ was all about. WWV weather warnings spoke of intense squall activity in our area. It was an understatement. For three days we never saw a celestial body. Conditions varied from dead calm to gale-force southeasterlies with nothing much in-between. The Doldrums were anything but dull. We beat toward the south-southwest and hove to when the winds blew their hardest. All an optimist could say was that at least the searing heat of the previous week was over with.

Tara and Eric handled it all with apparent ease. Lenore and I bore the frustrations of headwinds and poor progress—and more sail changes than we could count. Friends have talked of sailing to the equator with NE trades and encountering SE trades shortly after entering the Southern Hemisphere. All this supposedly transpired with clear skies and a happy crew. Apparently the ITCZ goes through cycles of inactivity and hyperactivity. I can attest to the fact that when it is active it can nearly close the door to progress to the south. Unfortunately, it doesn't follow a timetable like the phases of the moon, and what you'll find is a gamble.

Wind Shadow's intended landfall was a tiny atoll called Tongareva (Penrhyn), about 850 miles south of Fanning. Its central lagoon has beckoned pearl divers and adventurers from all corners of the world. Our hopes were far less colorful. If the normal east-northeasterly trade winds had persisted we never would have approached the atoll, but southeasterlies had plagued us from the time we left the Doldrums south of Fanning. We altered our direct-route plans for French Polynesia and decided to visit the Cook Islands instead. Tongareva was about 600 miles from the main cluster of the archipelago. *Wind Shadow* was low on diesel fuel, and the ➤ 57 crew certainly could use a break from two weeks of close-reaching and beating to windward.

The low-lying island was a navigational challenge. We were fatigued from a long night watch as we entered the current-ridden pass at about 0900. All we thought of was a safe anchorage and much-needed sleep, but the chart told us to be careful. The average depth of the lagoon was probably over thirty feet, and jagged coral heads climbed vertically to within a few feet of the surface. These hungry pinnacles could tear the heart out of any vessel ill fated enough to collide with one. I was aloft at the spreaders pointing to these coral heads. We were powering upwind toward the anchorage. I will not forget the sound of the engine stalling and the look on Lenore's face as she realized how quickly we had to get sail set or the anchor over. Fortunately, I had left the forestaysail ready to hoist. It was set and drawing before we lost steerageway.

Wind Shadow balances well under this sail, as she surely proved. We continued to tack toward the anchorage and were met by what we assumed was a friendly pilot boat, coming to give us a hand. In broken English we were asked if we had permission to visit Penrhyn. I indicated that we had been blown off course, were low on fuel, and now had engine problems. The pilot told us we could not stay because government officials had flown in from Rarotonga and they insisted that all arriving vessels first check there to acquire a permit. After our two weeks of hard sailing that was not the welcome we had hoped for.

Much discussion ensued. The pilot allowed us to anchor long enough to take on fuel and repair the engine. The problem stemmed from a cracked sediment bowl which had allowed air into the fuel line. I replaced the glass bowl with a jam jar and bled the engine. The engine started and we were once again on our way.

The weather was squally and the overcast hid the coral minefield we had dodged on the way in. The seal on the jam jar leaked and air entered the system. The engine stalled again. Up went the sails—*Wind Shadow* left as she had arrived. But Murphy missed his chance; whoever protects foolhardy sailors must have guided us toward the right part of the pass.

Totally fatigued, we headed offshore. It was only later that I realized how foolish I had been not to insist on the chance to seek safe shelter.

Four years hence a somewhat similar situation arose and I understood all too clearly how dangerous being turned away from Penrhyn had been.

In a three-and-a-half-month period, since leaving California's Channel Islands Harbor, *Wind Shadow* had sailed nearly five thousand miles. The crew was looking forward to some extensive gunkholing throughout the tropical archipelagoes of the South Pacific. Tara and Eric were looking tan and happy, glad to be part of this adventure. Lenore and I kept reminding each other that we had actually sailed away and found Polynesia. We had all adjusted to the constraints of cruising as well as to those of simply living aboard. Our sloop had taken the wear and tear of the long passages well in stride. We began to feel that the changes in our way of living may have been the right choice after all.

CHAPTER 3

Polynesia

It is not easy to sail away from French Polynesia. They say it's cruising's "promised land." The people, the lagoons, and the mountains all seem to have a pristine quality, capable of exciting the most hardened soul. When we finally left, however, after several months of sampling anchorages in perhaps the most beautiful archipelago in the world, I was surprised to find our departure so effortless. *Wind Shadow* was headed west again, toward Suvarov and Samoa. We were not lamenting our good-byes to Tahiti and its neighbors. Possibly the intensity of the experience had numbed our senses. We were not oversaturated with tropical cruising. Palm trees still held our interest. There were other reasons for leaving the promised land.

They had begun to develop nearly six months earlier. We had sailed *Wind Shadow* into Rarotonga, the capital of the Cook Island Group that lies six hundred miles south of Tongareva. Our sloop had been at sea for twenty-three days, and by now thoughts of ice cream, cold drinks, and shore leave were overpowering. Tara and Eric looked forward to playing tag and running around on shore.

The formalities of entering the country and clearing through customs were simple. Our Q flag was lowered and the crew scrambled into the dinghy. Tara and Eric were the first ashore. They began to weave back and forth like drunken sailors. Lenore and I did the same. We had become accustomed to the motion of the boat and were disoriented by the stability of land. We swaggered our way to the little town of Avarua, ready for the pleasures of a first day in port.

Our landfall, however, seemed an island out of context after the halcyon nature of Fanning Island. Rarotonga is a British version of Polynesia. New Zealand shouldered the responsibility of aiding the emerging island country, and quite a bit of British tradition has been assimilated into the local life-style. The workday pauses for tea breaks, and the islanders replace native dress with Bombay bloomers and knee socks! For us the sight was certainly a cultural contradiction. However, no one there seemed upset over the changes. The ten thousand local inhabitants were moving into the twentieth century at their own pace.

We were surprised by the variety of goods available in Avarua—engine parts among them. There was also a special kind of tinned New Zealand butter—far better than the dehydrated stuff we'd been using—that was always on Lenore's shopping list after that. Once the ice cream and cold-drink lust had been satisfied, we went our separate ways in search of items needed aboard *Wind Shadow*. Eric and I had to find a fan belt, transmission fluid, and some electrical cable. We located it all in a well-stocked hardware store. Lenore and Tara were delayed, off in search of vegetables, books, and the post office, so we returned to *Wind Shadow* by ourselves.

When the rest of the crew returned, Eric volunteered to row in and pick them up. He was only five, but his water skills were those of a much older child. This was one of the family's major concerns. Our children could swim every bit as well and were as capable in a dinghy as children twice their age. It was important that we determine their boundaries.

Eric heard Lenore and Tara hail from the shore. He made sure his life jacket was in the dinghy, then climbed aboard. His weight was placed amidships and his agile body settled immediately into the rowing position. He pulled for shore with the confidence of a seasoned Jack Tar, backed water with his starboard oar, and gently came alongside the wharf. The children each took an oar and taxied their mother out toward *Wind Shadow*. The wind and chop made rowing difficult, but Tara and Eric were careful not to overpower each other inadvertently. Their long strokes and coordinated timing gave them the advantage they needed. Soon *Taric* was alongside, packages and crew safely aboard. Lenore was clearly content with the ride.

Father George, an atypical Avaruan missionary priest originally from

Holland, helped us reprovision. We had met him on one of his weekly visits to the harbor. He was kind enough to take us in the mission's truck to pick up our supplies, introduce us to the manager of a fruit-canning factory (who, in turn, sold us his products at terrific savings), and give us a guided tour of the island.

Tara and Eric enjoyed Father George's tales of island customs. At one point the Rarotongans reenacted a biblical episode that we were invited to watch. The Devil was dressed in a black wet suit. Tara told her brother that if he had to wear that in a place so hot he'd be pretty mean too. Father George's Christian ways have aided visiting yachtsmen and his own parishioners for over twenty years. We will not soon forget him.

Rarotonga does not have an all-weather harbor. *Wind Shadow* was anchored in a bight that was sheltered from prevailing trade winds, but when the wind backed to the north the anchorage became a washing machine. A week before our arrival two vessels had been caught in the harbor by a northerly. They pitched, rolled, and yawed as the gusts and large swells scoured the anchorage. One vessel swung toward the east as the other yawed to the west. With the extra scope paid out for better holding, they collided. Damage was minor until the rolling motion caused masts and spreaders to tangle. Standing rigging parted, spreaders splintered, and one mast was literally shaken out of the boat.

Also, the cyclone season was approaching. With it came the increased frequency of northerlies. It didn't take a meteorologist to realize it required us to sail six hundred miles to windward, against the westerly-setting South Equatorial Current. No one looked forward to that passage—and with good reason, as it turned out.

For five days waves broke against, aboard, and over *Wind Shadow*. Only iron-stomached Eric kept a smile and an appetite. He slept in the forepeak and seemed unconcerned by the rising and plunging bow. He awoke each morning refreshed. The rest of the crew had given up berths and tried to sleep on the cabin sole, where the motion was a bit more docile.

French Polynesia made the wet passage seem worthwhile. We entered a part of the Pacific that was neither empty nor lonely. Islands were spread like stepping-stones across an indigo lawn. Here we found the ➤ 63 reality about which many a cruising fantasy is woven. French Polynesia is a feeling as well as a place. And making a landfall at Bora Bora is a feeling hard to forget.

We headed toward the pass; it was early morning and the steep-sided island lay dead ahead. All around us were seabirds heading offshore to feed.

As we entered the obvious cleft in the reef, the depth sounder read one hundred feet. There had to be something wrong with it. The bottom was clearly visible and I was sure it couldn't be more than twenty feet away. The lead line confirmed the sounder's reading. The thirty-foot depth inside the pass created havoc.

I climbed into the spreaders for a better angle of view. Lenore was at the helm, and Tara and Eric were reading the depth sounder. The current was moving with us—a situation I do not like when entering a pass. The speed of the current increased our speed over the ground to about 9 knots. Steering was less efficient with so much of our speed being with the water rather than against or merely through it, and if *Wind Shadow* did run aground, the current would push us farther onto the reef. I was reminded of our landfall at Fanning Island. Lenore held her breath. I looked away from the hungry coral passing beneath the keel.

It wasn't really a difficult pass to enter after all. The extreme clarity of the water had fooled our senses. As soon as *Wind Shadow* was safely in the lagoon, the current dissipated. We all took deep breaths and looked around at perhaps the most beautiful atoll in the world. Ote Manu reached up toward the trade wind clouds. At its feet a fringe of lush green palms seemed to hold back the lagoon. Enclosing us was a ring of coral. The steep mountains were a backdrop for one of the nicest anchorages to be found anywhere.

We anchored, cleared with the local gendarme, and all four dived into the water. It was the height of the dry season and the lagoon was at its best. Each dive seemed to offer another reason to pinch ourselves to see if what we saw was real. Tara and Eric were fascinated by all the kinds of fish they saw. Between dives, I looked up toward the mountain silhouetted against the blue trade wind sky. White fairy terns flew up in the thermal drafts. I heard islanders singing somewhere onshore.

At Bora Bora, the author and his family explored their anchorage under water and above. Here they watch a graceful native outrigger, traditional to the lagoons of many Polynesian islands.

Polynesia should be experienced under the water as well as on the land. Clouds and palm trees are only half the picture. Beneath the surface of the lagoon at Bora Bora we found a hidden world where animals look like plants and fish are as colorful as flowers. Some scientists say that the mid-ocean realm is a biological desert, that most life clusters about the reefs of islands like these, and that there are complex interdependencies among the inhabitants. I wouldn't dispute any of it. During one afternoon expedition we were snorkeling over a coral patch and saw several large groupers clustered together. A tiny minnow was swimming into and out of the mouths of the large groupers, which were waiting patiently to have parasites picked from their gills. The relationship helps both the cleaner and the cleaned.

Many of our encounters in French Polynesia, and later as well, turned into science lessons for Tara and Eric. Lenore was handling the formality of a regular three Rs program. I tried to show some correlation between what we were doing and what was important to learn.

Eric and Tara liked to draw boats. Their knowledge of rigging and sail plans was surprising. During one afternoon dive in our lagoon we took a closer look at why and how *Wind Shadow* worked. Slowly treading water, we tried to keep our masks exactly halfway submerged. The topsides and rig of *Wind Shadow* appeared in the upper half of the mask and the underbody of our sloop in the bottom. We talked about her lateral plane, wetted surface, and rudder function. The children understood how forces in one medium interacted with forces in another. We talked about the air/ocean interface. Tara and Eric decided that their home was a very efficient machine. Lenore and I were pleased to see them respond to such thoughts.

French Polynesia was not perfect. There were problems. In our wanderings among the Society Islands—Bora Bora, Raïatéa, Tahiti, and others—we observed the growing pains. Most stemmed from overly subsidized culture; Tahitians, for instance, were struggling with the hardware produced by the industrialized world. Possibly dirt bikes and 200-horsepower outboard motors are a sign of success. Some might disagree. In any event, the islands like Tahiti that see the most tourists seem to have the most acute growing pains. It may be one thing to say that the old

Progress in Polynesia includes the innovative floating Library Program. This multi-hull carries six thousand volumes from village to village, as it navigates within the Raiatea-Taaha Lagoon.

ways seemed so harmonious with the surroundings and another to try and stay with them, once the cold drinks and convenience of mechanization have been sampled. How long will it be before there is TV in Tahiti? It is already there.

Endless Summer is a low-budget surfing film I recall from the early sixties. It was the first of its type to succeed in Hollywood. The film was made by surfers and starred neither Frankie Avalon nor the well-endowed Annette Funicello. The idea of perpetuating summer left a lasting impression on me. Polynesia gave us an opportunity to see what it was like to do just that—make summer able to last forever.

But at times even paradise gets too hot. During the really warm part of the day, from ten to two, we spent our time in the shade or underwater. Awnings, wind scoops, and *Wind Shadow's* large hatches were appreciated. Even Tara and Eric had a midday slowdown. Lenore sensed how debilitating a tropical summer could be.

A book called *Sisters in the Sun* was one of my heat-wave diversions. It was written by A. A. Helm and W. H. Percival, two European authors who chased adventure in the South Seas before it became a thing to do. The book describes two of the Northern Cook Islands, Palmerston and Suvarov. I was fascinated by uninhabited Suvarov. Lenore and I shared the book's adventures with the children. It was easy to decide where we'd head once the storm season was over.

SUVAROV, ISLAND OF SOLITUDE

Suvarov was a strange name for an island in Polynesia. It had been discovered in 1814 by a Russian naval officer and named after the famous General Alexander Suvarov. The tiny cluster of sand and coral eventually became part of the Northern Cook Group. For centuries it had remained an island too small, too low, and too devoid of fresh water to attract more than an occasional visit from passing native fishermen. At one time a trading company tried to establish an outpost there. The effort failed. Treasure was discovered on the island in the late 1880s, apparently part of the cargo of a vessel off course and lost on the barrier reef. The thought of finding more booty attracted still other luckless vessels over the years.

However, the island's real treasure was neither gold nor silver; it was solitude. A New Zealander, Tom Neale, did more than discover it. He used it to live a fantasy hardly imaginable in today's world. He lived a subsistence life-style in a self-imposed isolation that went on for twenty years, with intermittent journeys back to the real world. Infrequent visits from cruising sailors were Tom's only other company. We had the good fortune to read the book he wrote about his experience on Suvarov. *An Island to Oneself* gives a very thorough portrayal of what isolation is all about. A sailor crossing a lonely ocean can understand these things.

The thought of sailing to Suvarov left us with some uneasy feelings. How could we intrude upon a man who had gone to those lengths to be alone? Cruising sailors who had been there before reassured us that he did enjoy occasional company. We were enthralled by the thought of such an adventure. Tara and Eric had already begun discussing what having an island to yourself would be like.

In Polynesia, the cyclone season is officially over on March 31. Cyclones have been known to disregard official seasons; in fair weather Suvarov is a good anchorage and in a gale it is terrible. In a major storm it is devastating. Seas have been known to wash over the low-lying island, and trees, as well as a yacht anchored in the lagoon, simply to disappear. We decided to pay close attention to WWV storm warnings, broadcast on 2.5, 5, 10, and 15 MHz.

In mid-March we departed Tahiti and headed west toward Suvarov. French Polynesia had been a chance to slow down and enjoy each day as distinctly different from all others. But it was time to leave paradise astern. The trade winds had stabilized. Our passage west turned into a fair-weather reach.

There is nothing like finding a tiny landfall in the middle of an ocean. Larger islands with mountainous peaks can be seen much farther away. An atoll with a diameter of eleven miles and a height of twelve feet can be elusive. We had heard of people who couldn't get celestial sights due to the overcast weather and never were able to find Suvarov. We also ➤ 69

The crews of Wind Shadow and Cara *share cruising tales while anchored at the* Papeete Quay, Tahiti. *The boats of friends like these became part of a "fleet"—met in safe harbors, spread across oceans, perhaps met again in later landfalls.*

knew of people who had clear conditions and were still unable to find it.

Still others found it—or other islands—in a way they did not mean to. Polynesia is a graveyard of nautical mistakes. We saw the remains of disintegrating hulks stranded high on surf-swept reefs. Most of these victims of the reef had succumbed to crew error rather than savage storm. The amateur yachtsman isn't the only one to err—commercial fishing vessels are parked upon reefs throughout the Pacific. Suvarov was going to be a good test of my celestial navigation skills.

En route to Suvarov we chose to sail by tiny Mopelia, a forgotten outpost of French Polynesia. The island was at one time the secret hideaway of the "Sea Devil," a chivalrous German pirate of World War I named Count Felix von Lueckner. He sailed his square-rigged *Seeadler* across the Atlantic, plundering Allied merchant ships, sparing their crews, and embarrassing the navies at war with Germany. When pursued himself, Von Lueckner escaped to the Pacific via Cape Horn—to continue his plundering out of Mopelia until a sudden storm drove *Seeadler* onto the reef. Von Lueckner was later captured, but after the war he outfitted the ship *Mopelia* to sail from New York to Polynesia, perhaps to retrieve some of the vast fortune he had plundered.

As *Wind Shadow* approached the pass on Mopelia's leeward side, we were confronted with a strong ebbing current. The tide was actually halfway through the flood phase, but strong trade winds and large seas washing over the windward reefs caused a continual ebb current here. As we closed with the entrance, I realized with a shock that the markers I saw were really the masts of ships driven onto the reef while attempting the pass.

Wind Shadow could hardly power against that current. If we broached in the narrow cut we could easily become another channel marker. As much as Mopelia intrigued us, we weren't ready to take the gamble. We were sadly disappointed, but fortunately there was Suvarov to look forward to.

It was a bright trade wind day, our fifth at sea since leaving Tahiti. We came about and left Mopelia astern, and began the westerly reach toward Suvarov. Three days later, as we neared the island, it became clear we could not reach it before dusk. New landfalls, even well-marked ones, can be dangerous to enter in the dark. Negotiating an unmarked

➤ 71

pass on an unlit island was something I would normally not even consider.

We decided to take advantage of the fair breeze and take a look at the pass when we reached Suvarov. A Yankee forestaysail and full main kept *Wind Shadow* moving at hull speed. Lenore reread every description of Suvarov we had aboard. There was a reef just inside the pass itself that under midday lighting would be obvious. But with the glare of the afternoon sun—even with polarizing sunglasses—we'd be unable to see much below the water's surface.

The *Sailing Directions* described natural landmarks in detail. We established danger bearings to help us as we made our way into the pass. If all went well we could be there with enough light to make a safe decision. If there was a current like the one at Mopelia we would sail well offshore, heave to for the night, and hope to return under better visibility the next day.

Tara and Eric were good lookouts. Even though Tara seemed to dominate "land ho" contests, her younger brother remained an eager competitor. It was about 1600 hours when I heard a puzzled conversation begin on the foredeck. Tara said that just off the port bow bushes were "growing out of the ocean." It was a good time to elaborate upon the effects of the earth's curved surface. Both children seemed to understand— Suvarov's palm-tree tops were the highest aspect of the island, so we saw them first.

It had become a close race. Suvarov was in sight and we were charging toward it. The sun was low in the west, daylight very limited. When we got to the pass the sun was balanced on the horizon. The trades had diminished and the current was nearly slack. We could distinguish an islet called One Tree Motu and other landmarks, and took bearings on the charted ones.

There remained one problem. We could not see the shoals without overhead sunlight. Twilight is short-lived in the tropics. The decision had to be made immediately. When darkness set in we had to be either safely anchored or on our way offshore. The current and all other conditions except that one were ideal for entering. Lenore and I discussed the options. The decision was left to the skipper. I weighed everything. Neither choice was optimum.

I made the difficult decision. Lenore, Tara, and Eric took positions on deck and we dropped sail for the approach to the pass. The sun was below the horizon by now and twenty minutes of twilight remained. The depth sounder showed one hundred feet, which would soon shoal as we entered the inner pass.

I noticed a larger-than-usual swell approach from astern and realized this was the bit of luck I had hoped for. Years of surfing had made me aware of the relationship between depth and the shape of waves. The swells passed gently beneath *Wind Shadow*, radiating into the pass.

The swells were as good as sonar. As they reached what had to be the shoal area of the reef, they changed dimension. Each became steeper and its forward movement slowed. They finally broke, indicating very shoal water. The reef was just where our bearings said it should be.

As we inched our way into the lagoon now, Lenore took the helm and I climbed aloft to the first spreaders. The angle of view was better and I could just make out the confines of the reef. Once past the danger we turned to starboard, motored up into the lee of a little island, and dropped the hook. It had been too hectic a day. I felt the elation of another safe landfall. All we wanted now was dinner and a good night's sleep.

The sun was well up before anyone stirred aboard *Wind Shadow*. We felt strange. We were no longer at sea, yet we hadn't entered port. It took a while to accept the fact that we had reached Suvarov. Tara and Eric scrambled about the deck, stowing sheets, blocks, and other gear used during the passage. I hauled up the anchor and moved to a better location before going ashore; we had been in thirty-five feet of water, and despite our six-foot draft it seemed as if we would touch the coral bottom.

Ashore, there were no footprints. The beach glistened. Tom Neale's boathouse looked as it had in his book. Quietly we made our way up to his dwelling, wondering what we would encounter. Our calls of hello were answered with silence. Closer to the clearing, we heard noises. A flock of half-wild chickens scurried into the underbrush. The coop gate was open. Once more we called and again there was no answer. I saw a paper attached to the door of one of the shacks. It stated that Tom Neale had left Suvarov three days before because of an illness. He welcomed ➤ 73

Saddened to learn that Suvarov's Tom Neale has, just days before, left for the hospital because of illness, the Naranjos accepted his hand-written welcome to strangers. Here are the islander's cook shed and a few of his pet chickens.

any visitors, offered them the use of his place, and asked only that they leave it as they had found it. Tom Neale was seventy-five at the time. We learned later that he had been hospitalized in Rarotonga with abdominal cancer and died within a few months of our visit.

We were disappointed not to meet such a special kind of person. However, the invitation to enjoy his island remained. We were the sole human inhabitants of Suvarov, a fact that grew in magnitude as each day passed. At first nothing seemed different. The weather remained consistently good. We established a routine, which featured flexibility. Time constraints were easily broken and there were no intrusions. Fishing and spear fishing replaced the market. Exploring became our entertainment. We borrowed Tom Neale's rowboat, put our 2-horsepower outboard on it, and set out to see the lagoon. Suvarov is a cluster of sandy cays, spread over a coral reef encircling the lagoon. We found bird rookeries, turtles laying eggs, and strange tropical plants. I could see why Tom Neale had so enjoyed beachcombing there.

Water was plentiful; Tom Neale had devised an elaborate roof catchment system to direct rainfall into large tanks. He had rigged up an outside shower as well as a scrub-and-squeeze laundry, and his house and separate cookhouse were meticulously clean. His life was obviously organized and at times must have been overpoweringly lonely. I could see how he came to love his island, but I would never envy his solitude.

Sharks seemed to enjoy Suvarov's lagoon as much as we did. We were careful to take a good look around before going for a swim. Several times diving for dinner turned into an unnerving encounter. One dive started with a concern over fish poisoning. Cigatura—a rare but deadly systemic disease—is caused by a toxic poison present in certain species of tropical reef fish. It may be linked to algae or plankton eaten by the smaller fish, but the toxin accumulates as it is carried through the food chain and some species of fish thus become hazardous to eat, even fatal. We normally try and eat only identifiable fish, known to be free of the toxin. I also prefer to avoid spearing overly large fish, even if they are easy prey, because they're likely to have accumulated more toxin. And, lastly, we try not to eat too much of the same species of fish.

We had been eating quite a bit of one type of grouper from inside the lagoon. It was time for a change of menu. I knew there would be more

Explorations of Suvarov included peaceful hours in Tara's coconut-palm playhouse.

diverse fish populations on the ocean side of the atoll, so I hiked across and worked my way out onto the reef, where I could slip into the water outside.

Visibility was astounding because of the lack of plankton, sand, and silt. Fish swam by in staggering abundance, unconcerned by my presence. Large bass, grouper, kingfish, and cavalli seemed suspended from the surface by strings.

I worked my way out from the ledge and surveyed the situation. The bottom sloped abruptly from ten to twenty feet and from there a coral plateau reached seaward. I looked carefully around for sharks but saw none. The situation seemed safe enough, so I hyperventilated and dived toward a medium-sized sea bass. Just as I fired the spear gun, the fish moved. The spear hit but did not kill or stun it. The bass wedged itself under a ledge. I had to surface for air.

As soon as I had taken a few quick breaths I returned for my spear gun, spear, and, it was hoped, fish. My initial tug on the spear was fruitless. Swimming to the ledge, I was astonished to find a black-tipped reef shark of about five feet doing its best to pull the bass out the other side of the ledge. I released the gun-to-spear connector, returned to the surface, and pondered what to do next.

The shark wasn't a dangerous kind, but I usually followed a "when sharks are around I'm out of the water" philosophy. The spearhead and shaft were the last ones I had. Possibly I could retrieve them once the shark dislodged the bass. I decided to wait for a few minutes and see what happened.

The shark suddenly pulled the bass free and took a ravenous bite from the side of the fish—and the tip of my spear was part of the hastily consumed mouthful. The distressed shark twisted and shuddered as it tried to dislodge the shaft. I noticed an immediate change in the behavior of the larger bass and groupers nearby. Their interest and activity increased. I turned to see how far I had to swim to get back to the coral ledge. From out of nowhere appeared a large light-gray shark. It swam directly over and fiercely attacked the reef shark. It was a mako, over ten feet long, and my being there was definitely a mistake. Of times like this the diving manual says, "Casually ease yourself away, without any splashing." After seeing the belly of the black-tipped reef shark ripped open, I was surprised I wasn't airborne. All I could think of was full speed ahead. ➤ 77

Tara, Eric, and Lenore explore one of the outlying islets encircling Suvarov's lagoon.

Sharks are a natural part of the tropical lagoon habitat. Avoiding close encounters means leaving the water when a shark is sighted.

As I reached the ledge I vaulted out of the water. That was the end of my spearfishing at Suvarov.

Tara and Eric had a better day. They explored our *motu* (our small coral island) and discovered a wonderful array of land crabs. The large, multi-colored, tree-climbing coconut crabs were the most unusual. Eric's favorites were the thousands of hermit crabs he saw, so he began collecting pets. Lacking something to carry them in, he filled his shirtfront full. It was a hard way to discover that the one oversized claw wasn't simply decorative. He said he was really lucky he hadn't put any in his pants!

The next day Eric and Tara wanted to explore one of the wrecks that had apparently found the island the hard way. It was an Oriental fishing vessel, one of the many that roamed the Pacific in search of schooling tuna. The little ship was high and dry, resting on her side, washed to this point by a storm sea. The tide barely lapped at her hull. I couldn't help but think of her captain's despair in losing a vessel this way. I pictured how it might have happened. The deck watch couldn't hear the breaking surf. The navigator made the first error, and the helmsman and deck watch could not react in time. With a grinding lurch, the vessel drove herself onto the coral. The ship was dead, the crew castaways. The story repeats itself time after time.

Suvarov also made all of us think about being alone. Our days had become less and less organized. Social time constraints had no meaning. We realized what a lone individual might have endured—the times of depression must have been intense. After only two weeks Lenore and I had come to understand much about an island subsistence life. Suvarov would not be our first choice for a place to live, we decided, but then neither would Manhattan. Somehow our attitude toward the "earn more to buy more" life-style had changed. Cruising had taught us that time for doing things as a family is a commodity beyond price. Sharing pristine, natural experiences here was that kind of time. We owed much to our two weeks at Suvarov.

Samoa, Tonga, and Fiji

When we departed this lovely solitary island the sky was clear and the trade winds were consistent. Another boat had just arrived. At first it was nice to have company, but their presence changed things. Two boats can be a crowd at a deserted island. After bidding farewell to the newcomers, I headed *Wind Shadow* west toward Samoa.

Before nightfall we began to encounter extremely steep seas, spaced very close together. I knew all too well what this signified—strong winds not far northeast of us. WWV weather warnings pinpointed a tropical storm about 250 miles from us, heading southwest at 10 to 15 knots. On our course we two would meet in about two days.

Early-evening WWV upgraded its warning to full cyclone status. The storm, named Robert, had 85-knot winds in its center and was expected to intensify.

Encountering a tropical storm at sea is the dread of every passage maker. Cyclones, typhoons, and hurricanes are different names for the same weather phenomena—they originate in warm regions near but not at the equator, intensify as they mature, and work their way toward or well into the world's temperate regions. They dissipate over land, and over water they can regain strength and keep rampaging for weeks. Fortunately, they are a closed spiraling circulation and their diameter isn't usually extensive. You can often avoid the worst of the storm by maneuvering toward its safe semicircle.

Lenore and I felt very apprehensive about the storm. Most cyclones in this region tend to move in a southeasterly direction, but this storm was moving southwest. I needed more information before I committed all of us to an evasion tactic. An amateur radio operator put my emergency call through to Fleet Weather Central in Honolulu, and a meteorologist gave us some vital information—satellite photography showed the storm to be undergoing upper-level changes that indicated a movement to the more normal southeast direction. *Wind Shadow* thus retained her westerly course to put as much distance as possible between the storm and ourselves. Even with reefed main and small staysail, we were sailing at hull speed and surfing wildly down the faces of large, dark swells.

The meteorologist had been right. The WWV broadcast twelve hours later said the cyclone was now headed southeast. Our dismal earlier thoughts about a cyclone at sea gave way to comments on the importance of having such vital weather information.

Two months later we met singlehander Eilco Kasemier. He had sailed his forty-foot ketch *Bylgia* in the 1976 Ostar Race—she has a quarter-inch rolled-aluminum-plate hull and is the strongest, most overstructured vessel I have ever come across, and a good choice for the passage he undertook. After the race he continued south, rounding Cape Horn from east to west and encountering thundering seas, icebergs, and overcast skies. Yet his worst day at sea had been "twenty miles from Tahiti." We had missed the full effect of Cyclone Robert; he had not.

Our next landfall was Pago Pago, American Samoa, which reflects good intentions gone astray. Somehow, federally funded programs had missed their target. Traditional Samoa succumbed to canned food, color TV, and an onslaught of other out-of-context products. Well-meaning bureaucrats had moved the values and hardware of middle America to the heart of Polynesia, but what was good for Kansas City was a disaster for Samoa.

A closer look clarified the sad problem for us. I was doing some research for an article about the changes that the island was going through. Misapplication of funds as well as ideas seem to pervade here. The half-sunk plywood fishing boats I saw were the last remains of a grant program that might have worked somewhere on the Great Lakes but was doomed before it got started in Pago Pago. The program established a boatbuilding effort here, but the vessels were not seaworthy in Samoan waters. Boats sank, engines malfunctioned, and very little fishing was done. The administrators never noticed that the Samoan preferred to fish from a canoe anyway and wasn't interested in the offshore populations of tuna. When we arrived the fleet was derelict, boats lay abandoned, and the fishermen had gone elsewhere. We stayed in Pago Pago long enough to receive mail and to reprovision, and then set sail for Tonga, six hundred miles to the south. All in all, American Samoa left us with a feeling of despair.

Vava'u, Tonga, was a refreshing alternative to Pago Pago. The people lead a predominantly subsistence life-style and seem to cling to many of the traditional ways of Polynesia. Their seafaring spirit has survived.

Tonga is the last kingdom in Polynesia. Its people are proud of their heritage and unharmed by the lack of overseas subsidy. We enjoyed talks with them on our explorations ashore.

Missionaries had established active outposts in Tonga some time ago. ➤ 81

Undergoing a complete refit in Pago Pago, American Samoa, is the handsome brigantine *Varua, owned by the famous sailor William Robinson.*

Polynesian Christianity was filled with vocal harmony and goodwill. The Tongans themselves have a valid means of determining which religion is the best. Last year the Wesleyan Church was the spiritual leader, we learned, but this year the Mormon Church had the most trucks for the islanders to use, the best celebrations, and the biggest following. It was fascinating to see how certain religious modifications had been made.

A young Tongan girl working in Samoa had asked us to take some gifts to her parents. We had met her in Pago Pago and were of course glad to do it. Her family—the Kaiheas—were a warm, friendly clan intent on expressing their appreciation for the gifts we had delivered. They showed us their island and introduced us to the delicacies of their diet—which included roast pig and taro root. Tara and Eric stayed overnight with them and played tag with the village children. Mele Kaihea—another daughter—spoke English very well. She had been worried that our reserved, quiet daughter had not enjoyed her visit. (Tara had indeed!) To the contrary, Mele said, she knew our wild son had had a great time.

The sail to Fiji, just west of Tonga, changed our cultural interests back into fairly strong concerns over seamanship. The passage is complicated by strange currents, hidden reefs, and overcast skies. It can easily be a navigator's nightmare because of the low-lying Lau Islands—the first part of the Fijian archipelago encountered coming from the east. Most cruising-boat navigators rely upon celestial navigation; there is no Loran coverage in the area, satnav remains prohibitively expensive, and RDF beacons are scarce.

Aboard *Wind Shadow* I updated DR positions with celestial fixes. I believe in navigational overkill. Rather than limit myself to a couple of sun sights and an advanced line of position, I regularly used stars, planets, and the moon as well. It may take an extra half-hour to do the extra celestial work, but I figure that someday that small expenditure of time may save *Wind Shadow* and the crew.

We had several days of overcast en route to Fiji. A couple of partial breaks in the sky gave me the sun sights I needed, though, and a near-full moon and a good break in the nighttime cloud cover gave us an accurate three-star fix. *Wind Shadow* had been set significantly off course by a southerly current.

➤ 83

We spent four months in the Fijian Islands, the westernmost boundary of Polynesia, before heading on to New Zealand. These archipelagoes mean different things to different people. For us aboard *Wind Shadow* they bring back wondrous memories of the lagoons, the islands, and those we shared them with.

CHAPTER 4

New Zealand and
Australia

New Zealand, it turned out, offered most of what we had been looking for on our journey. We sought a place to refit *Wind Shadow*, to replenish our savings, to take stock. Our surroundings encouraged us to linger. We became official residents and participated in the country's special way of life. When the time came to leave we found it our most difficult departure, because sixteen months of sharing the Kiwi way of life had drawn us close to the people and their customs.

New Zealand is a land with an abundant coastline, a seascape with a green wooded backdrop, and an interior of equal loveliness. Its economy is stagnant and goods sell for far from bargain prices. But a quality of life exists there that far transcends materialism. There is harmony between people and place. As a sailor, I could understand what made Susan and Eric Hiscock choose to make the Bay of Islands their home. New Zealand was the first and only landfall to tame and nearly conquer our family's desire to keep moving westward.

Sailing to New Zealand in the first place was a difficult decision. In Fiji we realized that our cruising budget had drained our savings. Finding casual work overseas is not too much of a problem, but work permits for long-term, well-paying employment are constrained by a web of bureaucratic red tape. The prospects for long-term work in New Zealand looked grim.

In Fiji the cyclone season officially begins in November, which is also spring in that part of the world. Those contemplating passages south, as we were, had to be ready to depart before that. We sailed for New

Zealand in the spring, as soon as a favorable weather pattern developed. If we could not find the jobs we needed, we would have to sail east in the prevailing westerlies and return to familiar territory for our needed financial refit.

The passage south from Fiji can be a difficult one. To avoid the cyclone season a crew must depart before the Southern Ocean's spring gales have dissipated. A clear departure from Fiji doesn't guarantee a clear approach to New Zealand, either. The best advice is to make as fast a passage as possible. "The longer one spends at sea, the greater are the chances of getting hammered," as the old adage says.

Good fortune sailed aboard *Wind Shadow*. Eight days from Fiji we closed with the coastline of the Bay of Islands, Northland, New Zealand. Our passage had only light-to-moderate southeasterlies and we made the entire twelve-hundred-mile voyage on one tack. *Wind Shadow's* light-air efficiency was to be praised. The only iota of adventure during the entire passage came while Lenore was reading Tolkien's *The Hobbit* to the crew.

I was at the helm, trying to get the most out of a diminishing 10-knot breeze. Tara, Eric, and Lenore were assembled on the port deck engrossed in the escapades of one Bilbo Baggins. It was a sunny afternoon and the sea was smooth. Speechless, I watched the tail fluke of a whale rise no more than ten feet from the bow. The creature politely disrupted the reading group as it sounded next to the port quarter. As it surfaced again and inquisitively swam toward *Wind Shadow*, its true size became apparent. The cetacean was half again as large as our whole boat. It showed no signs of hostility and we felt no alarm, just awe at a creature so large yet so adept at moving through its environment. The passage maker then submerged; we four felt that our world was as phenomenal as that of Bilbo Baggins.

The Nine Pin was passed to starboard and we headed *Wind Shadow* toward the entrance of the Bay of Islands. The coast's rugged volcanic outcroppings looked almost fjordlike. The hills were clad in green from plenteous rainfall. Charts, cruising guides, and tourists' material had given us background for a "we've been here before" feeling. Opua, one of the country's official ports of entry, lay near the head of the bay. We went through our usual ritual of cleaning the cabin, coiling sheets, and covering sails prior to coming alongside the custom's wharf. What a relief to be there.

"Ahoy, *Wind Shadow!*," came the call from the wharf. There waiting for us were John and Olive Shanks and their children, Robyn, Murray, and Janette. We had met them some years before in California, heard them extoll the quality of their native New Zealand, and written them from Tahiti about our intentions. A local radio operator had relayed the time of our arrival. All five of them now met us at the pier with baskets of food and an outstanding Kiwi welcome.

Before they could come aboard we had to complete customs and immigration formalities. The inspectors were friendly and thorough. Drug smuggling has grown so spectacularly that they brought a dog aboard— trained to scent contraband. At first we were quite concerned about our ship's cat, Bosley; Lenore imagined that the visiting hundred-pound retriever would go wild in the cabin and we would all be arrested. Bosley resented the intrusion but was safely locked in the head, and the narc dog acted as if Bosley was not even there. Canine agents are raised with kittens to avoid such problems, we learned, and this dog alone has been responsible for nearly ten million dollars worth of drug seizures.

The customs dog may not have been interested in Bosley, but the port medical officer certainly was. Strict animal quarantine regulations exist in New Zealand. They are a rabies-free country and work at staying that way. Their livestock and agriculturally based economy require tight control. Bosley hadn't had shore leave in over a year, but he was an old, neutered male and as long as his rations were regular and life wasn't too strenuous, he didn't mind his confinement aboard. We signed a bond agreement guaranteeing the confinement; if he disappeared or was caught AWOL, he would be destroyed and we would be heavily fined. We preferred to stay out at anchor anyway, however, so the quarantine regulation was not difficult to keep.

The afternoon grew into darkness as we and the Shankses reminisced. It was wonderful indeed. John also gave us a good introduction to the country and the potential for employment. Jobs were available in the teaching realm, although a teaching permit wouldn't be granted without a work visa or resident permit, and the outlook for either of these was dismal. John offered his help nonetheless.

The next day another spring gale growled into the bay. *Wind Shadow* was well protected and securely anchored. We rowed ashore with the first signs of clearing to have a closer look at the small community. The coun-

New Zealander John Shanks and his family, who learned Wind Shadow's *arrival time from a local radio operator, were on hand for a welcome to the Bay of Islands.*

tryside has an agrarian storybook quality. Small, well-maintained cottages seem to have the right amount of distance between them. Boatyards smell of wood chips, linseed oil, and enamel paint. It was all a breath of fresh air.

Russell, where we anchored for our first few months in New Zealand, is a boating community nestled in a corner of the Bay of Islands. Matauwhi Bay is its neighbor. As Thanksgiving and Christmas came and went, cruising friendships grew. The local Russell Boating Club encouraged visitors to participate in its races and raucous gatherings.

Our family found that the bay was at its best in early morning. Dew and crisp, clean Southern Ocean air were a good elixir. A row toward shore one morning might gain the attention of only a few red-legged gulls. Another time it might attract a pod of porpoises swimming in close enough to be touched from the dinghy.

On trips ashore I'd usually leave the pram at the boating club dock and walk into town. A cobbly beach ringed the bay, and fruit trees grew in grassy verges near the shore. At the head of Matauwhi Bay, the proprietors of the Port and Starboard Dairy sold milk with cream on top for eleven cents a bottle and butter for forty-nine cents a pound. Food was inexpensive, but color TVs were not; we were surprised to find that they were indeed sold in the town.

Life-style value is, of course, a very subjective concept. Lenore and I thoroughly concurred in our respect and affection for the Kiwi way of life. Others we knew felt instead that the high price of material goods is a real deterrent to a good life. They regretted a "lack of sophistication," evidenced by the fact that television had been available for only a few years and could offer only two channels.

A remark by a good friend of ours, Lee Matthews, exemplifies how Lenore and I feel: Lee and his wife Anna Lee had flown from California to share some time there with us. We left Tara and Eric with the Shankses, and we all bought unlimited bus and rail travel passes that let us tour anywhere in the country for two weeks, on the well-maintained government transportation system. Beaches and bays of the Northland gave way to rolling grasslands, and to snowcapped peaks and the alpine slopes of the South Island. Near the end of our two weeks, Lee was discussing the fauna and flora of the South Island with a New Zealander sitting beside

Wind Shadow *lies safely in Matauwhi Bay, one of many secluded anchorages in the Bay of Islands.*

him on the bus. Lee's comment afterward was: "You know, when a local plumber can tell you about the field habits of endemic bird species, a country really has something going."

The New Zealand sailors and their boats reflect a similar awareness of their natural surroundings. Because of the frequency of vigorous cold fronts sweeping through, the Kiwi sailor must learn early to cope with strong winds and the influences of an ocean swell. His boat must be soundly built to be able to contend with regular rough-weather conditions. Anchors are heavier, chains longer, and chrome less frequently used.

Cost and the availability of materials are strong factors too. One out of every four families in Auckland owns a boat, we learned. Many boatbuilders use galvanized mild steel fittings in place of more costly stainless steel and bronze. Fiberglass and teak are good boatbuilding materials but are costly and aren't the only ones available to New Zealanders.

Production boatbuilding was just getting started while we were there. Most vessels were one-offs, built in small shops with low overhead. Builders seemed to prefer wood construction of a multiskin nature. Native Kauri pine and epoxy glue techniques afforded good strength-to-weight ratios and created interesting racing as well as cruising vessels.

Within a month of our arrival we had settled into the local life. Lenore had found a waitressing job and I became a liberated boat husband. I cleaned the galley and swept the cabin sole and found time to do a few articles for boating magazines in the States. Naturally, I also saw to it that Tara and Eric kept up with the math and reading work so diligently pursued until now with Lenore. I even extended their curriculum to take in the physical aspects of education. Each afternoon, we worked on "kinesthetic developmental skills."

All was going well until Lenore noticed the surfboard in the dinghy. I reminded her how effectively surfing leads to other balance-building activities. I assured her that Tara and Eric always completed their school assignments prior to our treks to the beach. It was all to no avail. A friend was building a house and needed help roofing it. I reluctantly volunteered to help build. Lenore retired from waitressing and decided it was her turn ➤ 91

On Lenore and Ralph's inland exploration of New Zealand's North and South islands, Lee Matthews offers a tidbit to a red-billed gull.

Alpine slopes of the South Island, with their snow-clad slopes and clear running streams, invited hikes and other explorations.

➢ 93

to go to the beach with the foredeck crew. Thus ended our experiment in liberation down under.

House building turned out to be a great experience. The owner, head carpenter, and I (alias Nail Bender) were all sailors. We had each skippered a vessel to New Zealand and seen good reason to linger. The house belonged to former schooner-owners and Californians Betta and Brad Heising, and was built like a ship. Strong native hardwoods with fine names such as *totara*, *rimu*, and *matai*—as well as silicone bronze nails— were used in its construction. The house would never make a passage, but it was anchored in as fine a cruising ground as could be imagined.

Tony, the head carpenter, gave me insights into the complexity of trying to stay in New Zealand. Like us, he and his wife were charmed by the life-style and had begun the bureaucratic battle to achieve residency. It was a contest of papers, forms, and interviews. The first hurdle was one of exasperation; months of going around in circles usually led nowhere and the casually interested gave up. Tony told me of the arduous efforts of a European millionaire who sailed in on his yacht, fell in love with the country, and bought a moderate-size lumber business. His enterprise employed a number of New Zealanders and seemed to benefit all involved. Unfortunately, he made a crucial error in completing the application for residency status. On the line asking for trade or profession he wrote "millionaire." His application was rejected. The government list of needed skills and professions did not include that of "millionaire."

There was, however, a shortage of science teachers. I had a background in education and a teaching credential in biology. To my surprise, job offerings were abundant even for a sailor with a Yank accent. Acquiring approval to do the needed work, on the other hand, was like beating against the trade winds in a Tahiti ketch. Letters of explanation, recommendations, and even personal appearances did not work. Two teaching jobs had to be refused because I could not get a work permit.

Four months of frustration slid by and time was running out. Our tourist visa was good for only six months. The season for sailing away was near and we had no alternate plans yet. The twelfth formal letter from the government said that if I acquired a resident permit I could teach. The thirteenth letter stated that to be granted a resident permit I had to have a teaching job.

Tara and Eric race across a sandy stretch of Australia's Great Barrier Reef. Afternoon shoretime was a diversion all crew members looked forward to.

Bosley became an important part of the Wind Shadow crew.

All crew—including Bosley—enjoyed Christmas aboard in French Polynesia. Here Tara and Eric decorate a tree that took two days to find.

Tara and Eric sample tropical water as dinghy-handling skills improve in Hanalei Bay, Kauai, Hawaii.

Tara, Eric, and their father share the wisdom of Captain Slocum while living a few adventures of their own.

Wind Shadow *anchored beneath Bora Bora's volcanic peak, Ote Manu.*

Caribbean trade winds are most consistent in channels between islands. Wind Shadow and crew bound for St. Vincent, Windward Islands. (MIK MADSEN)

The author and his students from Henderson High School climb Mount Ruapehu as part of an outdoor-pursuits center experience in New Zealand.

Porpoises swim in Wind Shadow's *bow wave.*

In a Tahitian lagoon, with Moorea in the background, Tara and Eric discover how to use a snorkel and face mask as a new world unfolds before them.

Lenore, Ralph, Tara, and Eric Naranjo are a family alone on a deserted island—Suvarov—hundreds of miles from any neighbors.

Lake Wakatepu, surrounded by New Zealand's Southern Alps, is sheep-ranching country. Trout fishing and ample solitude seem dominant assets of the area.

Being ice-bound in the Chesapeake is not fun. The author counters the effect of an ice floe by setting an anchor to windward and kedging Wind Shadow *to safety. (L. D. NARANJO)*

This sunset in the Pacific was one of the glories of Wind Shadow's voyage.

Bahama Star *is shipwrecked testimony to the effects of wind and sea and to the vulnerability of inadequate ground tackle.*

In all Wind Shadow's voyaging, the creatures of water, land, and air were a delight to her crew.

A sea urchin and fish—New Zealand

An elephant seal—
Channel Islands, California

A snowy egret—Georgia

Three impalas—Zululand, South Africa

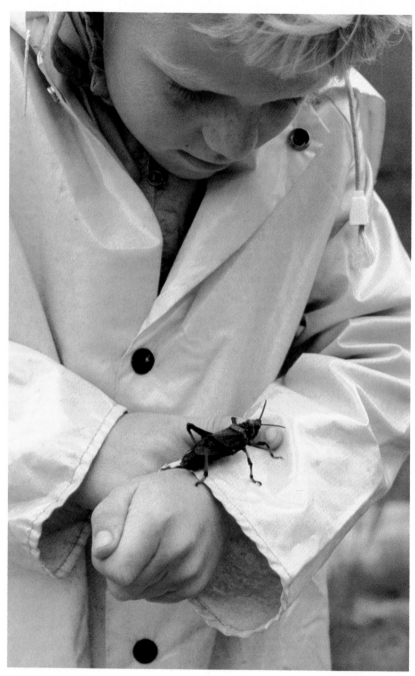

A grasshopper and Eric—South Africa (Drakensberg Mountains)

John Shanks and I made one last appeal. I had a science-teaching job offer in writing and sent copies of the last two contradictory letters to both the Ministry of Education and the Department of Immigration. The approval came just as we were planning our voyage back to the States. In a little over a week I would begin teaching at Henderson High School, about one hundred miles south of the Bay of Islands.

Shifting gears is part of life for the cruising family. We said good-bye to friends in Russell. Tara and Eric had been going to the local school and enjoyed the barefoot, carefree rural attitude. We prepared to sail south to a suburb of Auckland, the country's largest city. It looked as though *Wind Shadow* could be anchored near the town where I would be working. Summer was over and the fall gales can be uncomfortable, but the North Island's east coast abounds with sheltered anchorages.

Auckland turned out to be a rather rural city. Greenhithe, where we hoped to stay, was about eight miles upstream from where the Waitemata River empties into the Hauraki Gulf. Heading upriver, we felt full of anticipation. Tree-clad banks gave a rustic feeling to the estuary. But a strong current ebbed with the tide and the holding ground upriver was poor. The prospects for simply anchoring were dim.

Luckily, a sailmaker/carpenter/wonderful friend named Christine Hall, whom we had met in Russell that summer, rowed by and offered what turned out to be an invaluable suggestion. A chap who lived nearby might be able to help us.

When I met Lex Lundmark, he was charging a bulldozer headlong into a mass of pine-tree limbs and flames. It was early evening and the scene had overtones of Dante's inferno. Lex was clearing some land to build on. We were introduced. His handshake was as firm as his expression. I told him about *Wind Shadow* and my family. "You can stay on my float," was his response. I offered to pay for the dockage, but he refused. I felt profoundly grateful.

Among our neighbors in our new life in Greenhithe were Ross and Minine Norgrove, native New Zealanders who had spent years cruising the South Pacific and Caribbean aboard their schooner, *White Squall II.* They returned to New Zealand—Minine to remodel a house nestled in the pines on the point of Hearld Island, and Ross to become a writer. Our evenings with them were filled with sailing stories. Ross had been a

➤ 95

Sailmaker-boatbuilder-philosopher-friend Christine Hall, who made Wind Shadow's *storm trysail and helped the Naranjos in countless other ways, here works on a sleek rowing boat in Greenhithe, New Zealand.*

Special among friends who helped and welcomed in New Zealand is Ross Norgrove, sailing author and former owner/skipper of the charter boat White Squall II. *With him here are Pat Matheson, an author as well, and Ross's wife, Minine Norgrove, shell collector and horticulturist extraordinaire.*

➤ 97

Master Mariner, skippering the ocean going tug the *Aucklander*. He told hair-raising tales of wintertime sojourns down to 50 degrees south to tow home disabled freighters. Lenore and Minine shared some gardening adventures and left the old seadogs to reminisce.

It seemed that Ross and I kept returning to the same point. Cruising was more contingent upon the spirit of the crew than it was on the cost of the vessel. Ross told me of all his Kiwi shortcuts to building a sound vessel for less. They were functional ideas, which worked—like using galvanized mild steel fittings in place of stainless steel and bronze. Ross greatly influenced my developing attitudes toward voyaging in a small vessel. Without the help of people like the Norgroves, Shanks, Christine and the Lundmarks, our voyage would have turned east after too short a stay in New Zealand.

Life on the river was very different from life in Tahiti. Frequent rain, swift current, and mud complicated things aboard. The river's slippery banks were the joy of our son and the bane of his mother. Each morning Tara and Eric would make their way to school with friends from the houses nearby. By afternoon, Eric and Tara and their mates needed some diversion. Games of tag or chase through the woods all too often ended with a muddy slide down the bank to the water's edge.

I also went to school. My commute here was a bit different from the one in suburban California. Each morning Lenore rowed me across the narrow river to await the Whenuipai bus. It meandered its way to Henderson—about a half-hour ride through suburban New Zealand. On clear, bright mornings birds sang and all was right with the world. When I was behind schedule, or when rain was pouring down and the current in the river was near its peak, I would remind myself of the sunny-day ideas about the quality of life and laugh at my gloom of the moment.

Teaching at Henderson High School was a totally new educational experience. A few days before my first day there, a friend of a friend made a disconcerting remark to me. He was glad to hear of our luck in acquiring the necessary permit, he said, but was sorry I was not teaching in a better school. The academic quality at Henderson was fine, but the behavior of the children had certainly eroded over the years. I recalled my role as a junior-high-school disciplinarian in southern California. Just my luck.

Fortunately, either my informant was thinking about the wrong school or Kiwis have been spoiled by having the best-behaved adolescents I know of. At Henderson and all other public schools in New Zealand, students wear uniforms, do their schoolwork, and treat teachers with a respect that is anachronistic in most U.S. school systems. I tried to determine what caused such a positive educational climate. It might be the country's rural, agrarian outlook or perhaps a less dominant media bombardment. Whatever the cause, both teacher and student benefit from the outcome.

When I had been at Henderson about four months, some of the students in my university-entrance biology class talked me into joining a field trip. It was to be an intensive eight-day experience that included skiing, ice-caving, absailing, and rappelling at the North Island's Outdoor Pursuits Centre at Mount Ruapehu. My mountaineering background was minimal. I was still climate controlled for Fiji. Apprehension crept into my thoughts but did not stay long, once we were under way.

The program was organized by New Zealander Graeme Dingle, one of the world's most respected alpine authorities, and was designed to develop self-reliance and concern for others in a group. Its instructors reminded me of the people we had crossed oceans with; they had left conventional life-styles behind. They communicated their affinity for the mountains.

During one afternoon's snowy climb up Mount Ruapehu I had a memorable talk with one of my students, Jane Stocks. She had been to the Outdoor Pursuits Centre before, and her skills and endurance reflected it. In school she was a good student, though quiet. On the mountain she was outgoing and enthusiastic—we talked easily of the center's many effects on her friends and herself. She spoke of becoming a teacher.

Two years before, Jane told me, their group had been crossing a white-water streambed when one girl slipped from a rock, lost her grip on the safety line, and was swept downstream by the current. She was caught by a snag and held under. By the time the instructor and the other students could reach her, she had drowned. The girl's father later took the adult version of the same course, unbeknownst to the instructor. He saw that safety precautions were excellent and that his daughter's death had been a

➤ 99

tragic accident, not the result of negligent practice. He did not sue the camp or the school because he understood the need of his daughter and her friends to be on their own.

The climb to Mount Ruapehu's summit had been exhausting. We all rested, shared some chocolate, and spoke of going for a swim in the hot volcanic-crater lake. Instead, we took our pieces of plastic and slid several thousand feet down the snowfield in a matter of seconds. The plummet was the opposite of the hard trek up. Today, years later, I still think about that day and New Zealanders' love of being outdoors. I hope Jane has had her chance to become a teacher.

During all the months on the river at Greenhithe, we were both settling in and knowing that the time for departure would come. We knew we would take *Wind Shadow* to Australia and beyond. Our earnings would fit her out well for the coming voyage. We'd have enjoyed adding a refrigeration system and a new outboard for the Zodiak, but engine oil leaks, V-drive problems, cooling-system troubles, and a few other engine maladies needed remedy first.

Lenore and I pulled *Wind Shadow*'s hefty 37-horsepower diesel with a block and tackle on the boom. We ferried it ashore in the wallowing dinghy and sent it out to a local machine shop for an upper-end overhaul. Westerbeke parts are hard to find in Auckland, but fortunately, the company used a Perkins block for our 4-107 model, and interchangeable British parts were available. Getting the engine back in place was no mean task. We rafted up to a friend's large ketch, mounted their hefty spinnaker pole on deck as a gin pole, and lowered the engine into its compartment. It was hard to accept the idea of having a newly rebuilt, reliable auxiliary. Surely other problems would appear sometime. They did, but fortunately, they were few and minor.

One evening several weeks later, when Lenore and I were lamenting the imminent expense of upgrading our ground tackle, we got a brilliant idea for this next refitting step. We needed a powerful Nilsson manual winch, 250 feet of 10-millimeter chain, and a custom-fabricated bow roller. I casually mentioned my regret that we didn't have some nonessential piece of gear to trade or sell to ease the deficit spending. We both got the answer at once. The new masthead sensors and instruments I'd never had time to install were probably just what the local ocean racers were looking for; they were far from necessary for us. Lenore gathered them up and carted them off for a fair bargain with some Kiwi skipper who could put them to better use. The funds they generated bought us our winch. Turning wind instruments into an anchor winch is definitely evidence of a cruising sailor getting his priorities together.

More projects followed. We repaired the dodger, installed new pump kits, and rebuilt the head. Lenore painted lockers, varnished, and kept smiling despite the hectic nature of the refit. A lengthy further list of tasks—from replacing a through-hull to relaminating the outside skin of the rudder—was completed while we were hauled for ten days at the Salthouse Brothers Boatyard. The yard specialized in one-off constructions of wood and fiberglass sailing vessels. Their craftsmanship was superb and their reputation attracted clients from all parts of the world. Even though we were "do-it-yourselfers" without much money to spend, the yard was most helpful to us. This was the first and only actual hauling during our five years of cruising. On several other occasions I used an ample tidal range to careen *Wind Shadow* or lay her against a pier to antifoul the bottom.

The school year ended with a flurry of exams and project conclusions aboard our sloop. Plans for the summer began with a return to Russell and the Bay of Islands, and a bit more part-time work to assist the cruising kitty. Near the end of the season we would pick a favorable weather pattern and make a dash across the Tasman Sea toward Australia.

We took our time sailing north to the Bay of Islands, for truly beautiful cruising in the Hauraki Gulf and along the Northland coastline, and reached the Bay of Islands soon after our friend Denis Brown returned from his voyage to Kenya. Denis had sold his boat *Ravensong*, it turned out, and was building a house. I volunteered to swing a shovel with him and his son. We worked and watched the bay and discussed passage making in the Indian Ocean. Tara and Eric played on the beach close by and *Wind Shadow* lay at anchor fifty yards offshore. Lenore had taken a job in a local gift shop. The summer slid by in a patchwork of employment, play, and preparation for heading west.

Wind Shadow is careened on a "grid" for bottom painting in the Bay of Islands. Scrape, sand, and paint in one twelve-hour tidal period: a hectic assignment whose rates (free) fit nicely into most cruising budgets.

A New Zealand mullet boat, once used for fishing but now out on a peaceful evening sail, ghosts along in Matauwhi Bay.

AUSTRALIA

Cyclone Henry interrupted our departure for Australia. The storm was a compact, fast-moving low with hurricane winds. In two days it moved from New Caledonia to the North Island of New Zealand—nearly a thousand miles of raging. We had returned to Auckland to clear customs and now sailed up the Waitemata River to find shelter. The wind stripped trees from the banks and cast them into the water around us. I imagined what would happen if one landed on the foredeck. It's one thing to suffer damage from a storm at sea, but to be sunk in a river by a tree might be difficult to live down.

Wind Shadow weathered the storm and we headed on via Great Barrier Island and Whangaroa Harbor. Both are superlative reasons to consider New Zealand the best of extra-tropical cruising grounds. A fair breeze finally came to carry us around the fickle North Cape. Then the breeze quit. Spidery cirrus clouds approached from the west. It was the classic symptom of an oncoming cold front.

A day later the barometer began to fall. Northeasterly winds increased. *Wind Shadow* flew toward Australia at hull speed and more. Our weather information had said that the fairly stable high would give way to a fast-moving cold front.

It was happening. Sea conditions deteriorated before nightfall on our fourth day out. I had set storm trysail and storm staysail, cleared the decks, and double-lashed the dinghy and bagged Zodiak. Lord Howe Island, off to the west, reported storm conditions with Force 10 winds. Our test of the storm trysail was at hand.

The wind stayed northeast and our flying progress continued despite mountainous seas. The self-steering gear coped fine with the conditions. I had made a smaller wind-vane blade and it functioned quite well until dangerous cross-swells required a helmsman's timing.

Later that night, those cross-seas from the southwest began to cause unstable irregular peaks on top of the towering northeast swell. Several of these misfits crashed near us, causing *Wind Shadow* to slew sideways in a cascade of foam. Green water broke on deck with an ominous sound. As I went below to add another sweater under my sea-soaked foul weather gear, *Wind Shadow* rose up the face of an exceptionally steep wave. For an

With the hope of ice cream in the day ahead, Eric volunteers for an early bow watch as Wind Shadow *approaches Whangarei, New Zealand.*

➤ 105

Cape Reinga Light gives a bright navigational forewarning of New Zealand's rocky northern coast.

instant we were suspended with a significant port heel. The wave must have broken as we were hung near the crest. We fell into the trough with an avalanche of water instantly on top of us. *Wind Shadow* righted herself nobly and I scrambled on deck to see if the mast was still where it belonged. It was. A port was cracked, the dodger had been smashed, and several lifeline stanchions had been bent, but all else was intact.

At this point we were running before the northeasterly at about 6 knots. The storm staysail was already down and all we were carrying was the trysail. We were all right. The speed gave *Wind Shadow* good steerage and seemed to cushion the effect of the breaking seas.

The front passed through before daylight and we discovered what could be worse than a Force 10 northeasterly; it was a Force 10 westerly, a fierce and contrary wind that made us relinquish the mileage we had worked so hard to earn. For two days we remained hove to, only to be blown back where we'd come from. Finally, the breeze moderated and backed to the south. The sun and the porpoises returned, and our spirits rose. The passage to Sydney, Australia, would rank as our all-time "least-enjoyed" voyage. Anyone contemplating a Tasman Sea crossing, we decided, should consider doing it in a 747.

The Haven of Sydney

It took a full day to clear through the red tape of Australia's health, immigration, and customs services. We didn't mind a bit. We were out of the Tasman Sea and for the moment that was all that mattered. The Cruising Yacht Club of Australia made room at their dock for us and in their club facilities as well. We dried out, got *Wind Shadow* in order, and started exploring. Rushcutter Bay was close to downtown Sydney and a convenient place for becoming acclimated to city life. We visited the Sydney Zoo, which abounds with intriguing marsupials, and spent whole days at the Sydney Museum. We gazed at Sydney's beautiful opera house.

Several short-term work opportunities presented themselves in Sydney, and since we were too early to make our way up the Great Barrier Reef we decided to stay right there for our month's wait. My new role was that ➤ 107

Sydney was a haven after the struggle across the Tasman Sea, New Zealand to Australia in Force 10 winds. The opera house appears in the background, surrounded by Sydney's Jackson Bay.

of house renovator. Tara and Eric received a double dose of correspondence lessons for the weeks of hookey played as we crossed the Tasman Sea.

One problem remained. Liveaboards were frowned upon—especially those who were not at a marina but at anchor around Rushcutter Bay. There is a fine line between "visiting yachtsmen" and "liveaboard nuisances." If we anchored discreetly, in an unobtrusive corner of the bay, a month-long visit might not be too objectionable. We found the perfect spot—a tiny cove with only one house secluded on the hillside.

The first few days of house renovation went smoothly, and my employer decided that all Yanks must have strong backs and weak minds to work as hard as they did. I felt I was lucky to have a chance to work; the revenue meant better provisioning for the five-thousand-mile voyage across the Indian Ocean to Africa, and it allowed us options once there. I attacked the building's crumbling old plaster walls.

One afternoon Lenore rowed over to the yacht club to pick me up after work. As we headed toward *Wind Shadow* I asked if she had figured out what kind of flag was flying from the pole in front of the lone house on the hill. She didn't know, but she had seen a uniformed fellow in a powerboat circling *Wind Shadow* that afternoon. I felt like an illegal alien who discovers that the sheriff is in the neighborhood.

That evening we were hailed by the crew of a vessel that had maneuvered alongside. Instead of being arrested, we were invited, by formal invitation, to cocktails at the house on the hill. There was one problem, however. The engine noise had drowned out so much of the conversation that we weren't sure who resided in the formidable-looking dwelling.

We arrived for our engagement with minor trepidations. The house was grand indeed. Our intent had been to maintain a low profile. It seemed to have failed.

A steep staircase led us through a well-manicured garden into a spacious veranda. At one side stood a tripod holding an intimidating set of binoculars trained on the bay. I felt like a goldfish. Moments later we were introduced to the wife of the rear admiral of the Australian Navy. We had secluded ourselves in the most strategic spot in the entire bay. Our tans hid our embarrassment, I hope. We were soon joined by the rear admiral and fumbled through a couple of hours of very polite conver- ➤ 109 sation. We did eventually feel able to relax, though, and will always appreciate the cordiality and diplomatic way of the Australian Navy. I wonder what would happen to an Australian jackaroo if he decided to pitch a tent on the lawn of the Pentagon.

Soon our month was up and on we sailed, north from Sydney toward the Great Barrier Reef. Stops in Broken Bay and Port Stephens, New South Wales, made it clear that this coastline had some wonderful cruising grounds. We stayed awhile. Lenore, Tara, Eric, and I all decided this was among the best coastal cruising we had ever done.

Each morning, kookaburras sat on *Wind Shadow's* spreaders and awakened us with their ludicrous cackling calls. Our hikes through the bush were filled with marsupial encounters. Wallabies and kangaroos are strange beasts—their grazing habits are similar to larger herbivores, but their way of moving is certainly different. All we could imagine was a three-hundred-pound jackrabbit going thumpity-thump. Tara and Eric chased after the biped pogo sticks with little chance of catching up. The birds were diverse and beautiful—cockatoos, currowongs, rainbow lorikeets, and kingfishers among them. We carried a field guide and tried to learn what avifauna we were seeing. Even Eric, whose preference in winged flight tended toward the F-111, took a keen interest in these coastal birds.

Our voyage north to the Great Barrier Reef was soon at hand. It had a few exciting moments. The first began when night was near and it was time to head *Wind Shadow* offshore. I took a bearing on a lighthouse on Tacking Point. It was a strange name for a headland. I gave it no further thought. I gave it more thought after all when we closed with the coastline again at 10:00 the next morning. We were astern of where we had been fifteen hours before: Tacking Point was aptly so named by Captain Cook, who must have encountered the same combination of north wind and southerly-setting current that made our progress nonexistent.

We did finally get north. When wind and current were against us we explored an interesting harbor. With favorable winds we made some gains. When the next cold front went through we tethered *Wind Shadow* to the southwesterlies that followed it. Our progress up the coastline was splendid and the wide reaches were easy on the crew.

Our next bit of trouble came as we neared Coffs Harbor, about seventy miles past Tacking Point. The barometer dropped and the wind backed toward the east. Cumulus clouds thickened and rolled in from the south. A "southerly buster" was on its way.

Night came before we made port. The front overtook us and a gale-force southerly sped us on toward Coffs Harbor. I had a good chart of the entrance, but it was dark and conditions were poor. An Australian sloop near us was also apparently headed for Coffs.

Earlier, as the winds increased, I had begun to shorten sail. We had started with a full main, the genoa staysail, and the nylon drifter. The drifter came down and a reef went into the main. We ended up with two reefs in the main and no headsail at all. The wind was screaming, but the seas inside the down-coast current were slight. The Aussie boat ahead had dropped its headsail and continued under full main. His speed opened the gap between us.

Bearings I took on two coastal lighthouses indicated we were about two hours from the Coffs breakwater. I was extremely tired and had to get some sleep. Lenore took the watch and would wake me in an hour. I collapsed on my berth and was asleep moments later.

Off in the distance I heard a voice calling me. Sleepily I recognized it as Lenore's. Suddenly the words became clear: "We're going to hit it!" I shot through the hatch. If it had been closed I surely would have splintered through it. On deck I saw Lenore prepare to head *Wind Shadow* up sharply to avoid a collision. She yelled to me to look dead ahead at the piling we were about to hit. Miles away stood a hundred-ton crane, perched on the edge of the breakwater in Coffs Harbor. Lenore had problems with depth perception at night.

We both calmed down and I took the helm for the approach. The Australian sloop had entered well ahead of us. I dislike going into a strange port at night, but this one was well marked, we had a detailed chart, and the conditions offshore were going to get worse.

We made it with no further incident. Once inside we dropped sail and anchored, and I hailed the Aussie. We exchanged greetings and I commented on how fast a run he had had. He was single-handing and had been unable to get the mainsail reefed.

For the next several weeks we sailed peacefully northward inside the ➤ 111

Great Barrier Reef, in company with friends on another boat, and explored the coral coast of Australia. In Darwin, we both made plans to cross the Indian Ocean. Our friends took the high road and we chose the lower one. Their voyage would carry them on to India, the Red Sea, and the Mediterranean. Ours was the lumpy route to Africa and across the Atlantic to the Caribbean. Sadly we parted company in Benoa, Bali, toasting to each other's fair winds and good fortunes.

CHAPTER 5

Navigation and Seamanship

It is fair to assume that farmers have an awareness of the land, and that city dwellers are familiar with urban sounds and ways. Likewise an off-shore passage maker cannot help but come to know the sea. The greater the interaction with land or city or sea, the more complete these understandings become.

Looking back at the navigation and seamanship skills we set sail with, for example, and how they were sharpened by our five years of passage making, I've arrived at a few conclusions that seem worth passing on. They deal with making landfalls, understanding weather patterns, and developing an awareness of currents and sea conditions. Each skill influenced the safety of *Wind Shadow*'s passages.

The coral reefs of the South Pacific have claimed many a sound vessel. Most of these tragedies arose not because of violent storms but out of navigational inaccuracy. Being able to cope with a noon sight in a marina slip is not knowing all there is to know about celestial navigation. Nor are electronic aids a fail-safe alternative to sextant, almanac, and sight-reduction table; Omega units in our small fleet were unreliable, satnav systems were reliable but prohibitively expensive, and most of our cruising was beyond the range of Loran C. Our choice aboard *Wind Shadow* was, therefore, simplified. I became as familiar with celestial navigation as possible.

Robert Kittredge taught me much in his handy guide *Self-Taught Celestial Navigation*, a basic approach that downplays theory and stresses the "how-to" aspect of this mystical art/science. The book was written after a circumnavigation aboard his ketch *Svea.* I never met Mr. Kittredge, but we did cross wakes with *Svea* in Darwin, Australia. Her new owners Don and Sue Moesly were headed west on a circumnavigation of their own.

There are several good navigational formats for offshore cruising. Initially I preferred the H.O. 249 sight-reduction system. We sailed *Wind Shadow* across the Pacific with this method. In New Zealand I received by mail a TI58 programmable calculator with a navigational chip that allows it to function as a sight-reduction computer. The unit processes *Nautical Almanac* information, time, and sextant measurements that I furnish; stores and compares up to six sights; and yields latitude and longitude readouts for any two sights stored. The gadget eliminates minor calculations, thumbing through tables, and drawing lines of position on plotting sheets, but it is electronic and therefore vulnerable to the offshore environment. Surprisingly, I never had any trouble with the unit, perhaps because I was always ready to dig out H.O. 249 and my broken pencil.

Navigational techniques are objective, but their implementation is, of course, highly subjective. There is not much to run into between California and Hawaii, so it was a good twenty-three-hundred-mile passage for testing our own celestial navigation skills. I'd heard, "Just follow the jet trails and then turn your RDF on after two weeks." There is obviously more to a downwind passage to Hawaii than that.

During both of the California-to-Hawaii passages I saw very few jets. Visibility was generally a problem at the start. The first day's sunshine gave way to the dominant summer overcast of the outer Santa Barbara Channel. For five days we were forced south by a persistent westerly. I updated my DR plot with sun sights at every momentary break in the cloud cover. I calculated two or more sights to use the traditional "advance the line of position" technique—the celestial equivalent of taking two bearings on a visible landmark an hour or two apart. In the celestial application the earth's rotation must be compensated for, which the *Nautical Almanac* does by treating the celestial body as if it were actually moving about the earth. Sometimes I did a noon sight as one of the LOPs, but during June and July the sun assumes its most northerly declination, and getting a noon sight becomes tedious. Earlier or later in the year, when the sun is lower in the sky, measurement is easier and more accurate.

Wind Shadow's shakedown cruise to Hawaii presented no navigational surprises. Fanning Island, the lonely atoll hidden away in the Line Island Group, was a different story. The tiny island rises only about ten feet above sea level (Hawaii's Moana Loa is well over ten thousand feet) and strong current anomolies make reliance on DR very unwise. Fortunately, our approach coincided with good visibility. During the three days before landfall I used dawn and dusk rounds of star sights to add accuracy to my celestial navigation. I found it important to choose a twilight period where the horizon was still well defined. I preferred to shoot the brighter celestial bodies in the east, first, and then turn toward the western horizon. Planets and first-magnitude stars are the best alternatives, but there are times when you take whatever you can get.

We approached Fanning Island in a light wind. A round of predawn sights placed us fifteen miles or so north of the tiny atoll. Progress was slow. I generally kept engine use to a minimum because of the uncertain availability of fuel. Our sun sight at 1000 hours said we were about seven miles from the speck of sand and coral we were looking for. Before long, as mentioned, Tara and Eric sighted the cluster of green climbing out of the sea a point or two off the port bow. As we drew closer, our green mirage turned out to be the tops of the tallest palms on Fanning Island. These Pacific atolls are so low that cyclones and storm seas often sweep them clean of all vegetation. Finding such a landfall becomes more difficult.

The passage toward the Cook Islands, our next landfall, was dominated by shifting trade winds that put us uncomfortably close to Starbuck Island. That uninhabited chunk of coral offers neither lagoon anchorage nor sufficient lee. A coral mine field surrounds it and some parts of the reef reach out five miles to seaward.

The fix I had taken at dusk had placed us in a safe location; somewhere near midnight we would pass twenty-five miles safely to windward of the island. South-southwesterly winds and squally weather altered our plans. The best course I could sail now would bring us dangerously close to the hungry windward coastline.

It was a moonlit night. Between squalls enough horizon was discernible for another round of star sights. My earlier fix seemed to be a reliable one, but the *Pilot* mentioned strange current effects and I was concerned over Starbuck itself, so I was eager to update our position.

Small islands are difficult navigational targets. This one, unlike many others, has not lost its vegetation to sweeping storm seas, so its trees can increase its visibility.

Many authorities warn against taking star sights at times other than dawn or dusk. They speak of horizon inaccuracies and errors originating from the moon's uneven reflected light. I had tried the process for myself and found that if I could choose celestial bodies evenly spaced around the horizon, lighting ambiguities seemed to cancel out. I regularly took rounds of star sights during full-moon and near-full-moon conditions, and the fixes proved reliable. One technique I recommend for celestial sights incidentally, is omitting the telescope from the sextant; stars are so distant that their apparent size does not increase through the use of a low-power telescope. The boat's motion and the apparent movement of the horizon are all that get magnified.

Once I had recorded the altitude of several stars and planets as we headed toward Starbuck, I slipped below to calculate the fix and update our position. Lenore was at the helm and *Wind Shadow* proceeded under reduced sail. All vangs and preventers were free. The depth sounder was on and *Wind Shadow* was ready to come about at a moment's notice. The new fix and DR correlated reasonably well with the sights taken at dusk, but despite my knowing where we were, problems still lay ahead. If we continued to sail the best weatherly course possible, we'd still end up dangerously close to the windward side of the island.

We had three alternatives: heave to for the night, fall off to leeward of the island, or head northeast on the other tack. I trusted my fixed position so eliminated the last choice. Heaving-to would keep us in the area most affected by the strange currents and we'd still be to windward of Starbuck. We eased the sheets and headed to leeward of an island we were never to see.

A few hours later I was at the nav table figuring when we would pass Starbuck. My calculations showed we were about fifteen miles from the obstruction lying farthest off its shore. Before I had put my dividers away Lenore was giving me one of her "you'd better come on deck" alarms. Halfway out the companionway I smelled the unmistakable, pungent odor of a surf-swept reef. I checked the depth. We were safely off soundings. We listened for the sound of breaking waves. Nothing.

We were fine, as it turned out. Our olefactory senses were accustomed to the odor of the sea, and coral has a decidedly different scent. Starbuck's coral smell had traveled many miles toward us on the wind. The ➤ 117 experience was a good navigational test, but we had cut things a little too close. An island that can be smelled but never seen adds too much anxiety to a navigator's life.

CHARTS AND COMPASSES

Islands stretch across Polynesia like stepping-stones. Each new landfall gives rise to new navigational decisions. Before each approach, I tried to develop a realistic image of what to expect. Large-scale, detailed charts were my most valuable source of input. Next came cruising guides, *Sailing Directions*, and *Coast Pilots*. Aerial photographs, travel guide pictures, and comments from other sailors also yielded significant details.

For entry into a foreign country, I tried to choose an all-weather harbor. Commercial ports tend to have heavy traffic, but they usually offer better navigational aids and they are generally free of shallow obstructions. Before each landfall we'd evaluate each piece of information, combine these inputs, and then create a composite of our new port of call.

Nearing a coastline, I doubled up on navigational efforts. Dawn and dusk star sights became a part of our routine. I compared DR data with celestial fixes and established the effect of currents. Then if overcast conditions became a problem, I'd have as accurate a DR capability as possible.

I also utilized RDF beacons when they were available. I'm not overwhelmed by the accuracy of this kind of navigation, but when the fog closes in and there is no Loran, radar, or satnav aboard, it's an important alternative.

We discovered that navigational aids in most third-world nations vary between unreliable and nonexistent. Fortunately, there are reliable charts for most of these cruising areas. I have used French, British, New Zealand, Australian, South African, and American charts. I generally used the charts produced by the nation we were visiting, because they tend to be more accurate and to yield the most information.

Since we were unsure of our itinerary, we did not buy all our charts before departure. It worked out better that way, because sometimes I could trade charts with people who had come from the places we planned to visit. Since there were few navigational aids in many of these areas, we needed only minimal amounts of updating from the current *Light Lists*.

The depth sounder and the hand bearing compass were essential tools when it came to navigating in poorly marked, tight confines. Cruising inside the Great Barrier Reef of Australia proved both instruments invaluable. Bearings taken on the high points of small islands and their prominent headlands regularly updated our DR. Many areas shoaled gradually, and consecutive soundings became another source of good information.

Traditional bow and beam bearings on a single landmark told us how far away from it we were. We held an accurate course and began the distance calculations when the landmark appeared forty-five degrees off the bow. Tara and Eric helped, reading speed or time information. The measurement ended when the mark was exactly abeam. Since the forty-five- and ninety-degree angles created an isosceles triangle, the distance run was equal to the distance off the landmark. In bow and beam bearing situations, of course, the computer adage of "garbage in, garbage out" is a relevant precaution. If bad steering or a strong current throws off the speed/distance calculation, the results will also be inaccurate.

In our cruising along the Great Barrier Reef, two nautical tragedies drove home the value of careful navigation. The first was the tale of a sailor driven to disaster by his love of music and lack of common sense. During a refit he installed a set of stereo speakers in the cockpit. The magnetic compass had as much affinity for the new addition as the single-handed skipper did. Unfortunately, the compass deviation caused by the speakers' ceramic magnets caused the vessel to sail off course and collide with a surf-swept coral reef. The single-hander swam to safety; his vessel was a total loss.

Obviously, the compass aboard a cruising boat deserves serious consideration. For ours, I logged its deviation and checked it regularly. When we moved gear such as anchors and chain, or added electronic components, I checked the effect upon the compass by comparing compass bearings with celestial azimuths.

Sailing in the opposite hemisphere from where it was made can also ➤ 119 have an effect on a compass (some cards take on a drunken list known as "southern dip"). Flat, card-type compasses are more susceptible to problems from this phenomenon. Before leaving California, I made sure that our compass could be adjusted for such effects. I also checked that needed parts were readily available and found who supplied them.

The second disaster I mentioned was based upon navigational decision-making rather than mechanical error. During our passage up the Great Barrier Reef I learned a lot about the navigator who had originally owned the charts I used. A friend had given them to me in Sydney. He had said there was an interesting tale about the crew that had used them before, but I didn't hear the story until the subject again came up in Darwin, Australia.

The charts contained the pencil markings of the most thorough piloting I had ever seen. Bearings on landmarks were oftentimes taken at half-hour intervals and were meticulously plotted. The volume of effort was intimidating; until then I had considered myself a conscientious navigator, but compared to what was on those charts, mine was only a passive interest. In Darwin I mentioned this extreme diligence to the chap who had given us the charts. He responded with a tale of true irony.

It seemed that the charts' original owner safely exited the Great Barrier Reef and headed toward Nouméa, New Caledonia. He made landfall in the afternoon and began to sail his way through the convoluted passage among the reefs fringing the entrance of Nouméa. Three-quarters of the way into the harbor the crew realized it would be dusk before they reached the anchorage. There were range lights and reliable navigational aids, but the skipper chose to sail back out through the reefs and stay offshore until dawn. The choice turned out to be the wrong one. During the night, the vessel collided with the very shoals they'd successfully avoided earlier. The crew escaped to safety, but the boat became another monument to shattered cruising dreams.

As important as reliable instruments and accurate fixes is navigational decision-making. Once calculations are complete, a special phase of cruising takes over. It is a synthesis of navigation and seamanship. In larger vessels it is seen as an interaction between the bridge and the deck. For Lenore and me it began with discussion of the alternatives available.

Entering New York Harbor after the long voyage is over, Tara and Eric could help with watches by ages ten and eight. They keep a sharp eye out for freighters and ➤ 121 *tugs.*

Large breaking swells—antithesis of the flat trade wind seas—were a prelude to three days of stormy weather between New Zealand and Australia. Those days gave the Wind Shadow *crew a distasteful opinion of the Tasman Sea.*

Eilco Kasemeir, aboard his sturdy ketch Bylgia, weathered Cyclone Robert off the coast of Tahiti. Despite his passage east to west around Cape Horn, he felt his worst weather was encountered nearing Tahiti.

The final decision rested in the skipper's hands. I was the primary navigator; Lenore's obligations to the educational program and the health and welfare of the crew left little time to spend on navigation. Even so, she regularly double-checked my plotting and occasionally did some celestial sights on her own. It's important to have more than one person on board who is capable of navigating.

Quite early in our cruising I also learned how important it was for all of us to have a reserve of energy. This is a simple concept that basically amounts to keeping the crew as rested as possible. Emergencies require long-term output from a shorthanded crew, and disasters can arise from a seemingly inconsequential mistake. So Lenore and I tried to maximize sailing efficiency. We valued fast passages, but not at the expense of rest and reasonable comfort below. Eventually we learned to reef early enough and avoid most fire drills, yet late enough to benefit from a stiffening breeze. Tara and Eric shared many sailing chores. Gradually their input began to ease the load that Lenore and I had previously dealt with.

WEATHER

Another immediate concern of every passage maker is weather. You don't need a degree in meteorology, but a good working understanding of surface air masses and how they react with the ocean is essential. Equally important is developing an understanding of seasonal storm activity in various ocean basins. The British Admiralty's *Ocean Passages of the World*, which we referred to frequently, gives a good overview of these patterns. *Pilot Charts* depicts average conditions in specific weather sectors and are invaluable in determining when to make a critical passage. For general meteorological background we relied on authors such as Kotsch, Slocum, Watt, and Coles.

Most trade wind sailors avoid open ocean crossings during the cyclone season, which I feel is an essential part of good seamanship. Our Tasman Sea encounter with the Force 10 storm seemed about all *Wind Shadow* and crew could be expected to withstand. Breaking seas and fifty- to seventy-knot winds made capsize a distinct possibility. We were fortunate to be spared.

The mature cyclone Robert generated even more devastating conditions. Fortunately, most of these storms come only during summer and early fall; the rest of the year is usually free of them. Robert was, however, an out-of-season storm; we knew that the cyclone season in that region usually ends in mid-March and here was Robert in early April. As mentioned, we plotted Robert's projected course, checked and logged the barometric readings every half-hour, and agonized over conflicting weather information from WWV and directly from Fleet Weather Central on the SSB. The decision about evasive action was mine, and because I knew that most mature cyclones in this region head southeast I put my faith in Fleet Weather Central. It was a decision of more than minor implications and fortunately it turned out to be the right one. Robert developed sustained winds of well over eighty-five knots and was one of the worst cyclones to hit French Polynesia in twenty-five years. It was out of season, but the odds are still with those who have a basic understanding of weather patterns—and, as *Wind Shadow* did, make their passages in the off season.

The shorthanded crew has a special disadvantage in heavy-weather confrontations. Having someone at the helm can mean the difference between danger and disaster. A good self-steering gear can steer a fairly straight course even in extremely heavy weather, but it is a blind, unthinking helmsman and cannot react to the steep cross-swells that can break on the vessel's beam and roll it over.

A well-known boating illustrator recently did a piece on heavy-weather tactics. His sketches depicted storm seas marching in orderly ranks like eighteenth-century British soldiers. Such stylized storms are exceptions. In most heavy-sea conditions chaos replaces regularity. If possible I prefer to run before the storm under trysail and storm jib, angling down the face of cresting seas.

At times *Wind Shadow* harmlessly cascaded into a trough of a wave. The avalanche of white water would have easily rolled a vessel caught with her beam exposed to such energy. Under less dangerous conditions, heaving to with storm jib backed and the rudder hard over provides reasonable comfort and a chance for the crew to gain some needed rest. Again,

➤ 125

fatigue is one of the biggest factors in problems arising from heavy weather.

We also made the deliberate decision that for us, despite hurricanes, the safest, most enjoyable cruising would be found in the trade wind latitudes. Leave the Roaring Forties and Screaming Fifties to the Whitbread crews and enjoy the lagoons of Polynesia. Which indeed we did.

There were two weather indicators I paid especially close attention to. The first is the barometer; the second is cloud cover. The exact barometric pressure isn't as important as its tendency to rise and fall over a period of time. When the change is rapid, strong wind can be expected fairly soon. The strength of the breeze depends in part upon the pressure gradient over those waters. During our cruising, the glass once or twice rose fairly rapidly above the 1040 millibar mark and on several occasions dipped below 980 millibars. In each episode there was more wind than we wanted.

Perhaps the most bizarre of *Wind Shadow*'s weather encounters were the sunny gales. Certain regions of the world are known for these gusty conditions without a cloud in the sky—Santa Ana winds in California or the howling offshore wind of the Gulf of Tehuantepec in Mexico are two of these high-pressure paradoxes. They arise from too much of a good thing: an intense high, a steep pressure gradient, and an influence from the land. We flew before one of these sunny gales on a passage up the coast of New Zealand's North Island. The barometer had risen more than thirty millibars in a twenty-four-hour period and was nearing 1038 millibars—and still rising. The sky was deep blue and only a few fragments of cumulus clouds were left to remind us of the low that had moved well to the east. Staying close to shore minimized the wind's fetch and lessened the effect of the sea.

Cloud cover was a good way for us to tell what weather lay in the immediate future. For example, high-level cirrus is the forerunner of a frontal system. It is usually followed by stratus overcast and culminates with the approach of a dark band of cumulonimbus clouds, marking the arrival of the cold front—the more vertical the dark clouds, the greater the front's intensity. Once the front has moved through, light fractocumulos clouds appear with their scattered, cotton-ball appearance. Fair weather follows as another high-pressure system moves into place. We found the sequence repeated continuously in the temperate regions. By the time we reached Australia even Tara and Eric recognized the cirrus build-up warning of yet another approaching cold front.

We received regular and accurate weather information from several sources, the most important of which was a selective, sensitive multiband Sony receiver. Radio Shack and a host of other manufacturers produce this kind of general-coverage receiver with phase-lock loop tuning, digital readout, and continuous coverage from 3 to 30 Mhz. These units usually run on a separate twelve-volt power supply as did ours. A BFO (Beat Frequency Oscillator) allows single-sideband communications to be unscrambled.

Our receiver picked up weather broadcasts of even weak stations in fringe areas. We'd find the times and frequencies of local weather information in *World Wide Weather Broadcasts*, a government publication we'd gotten from Southwest Instrument Company before leaving California. The book also includes weatherfax data for those lucky enough to afford such gadgets, but the hard-core radio buff who has his CW code under control has an interesting alternative. NOAA broadcasts Morse code surface analysis regularly all over the world. Numbered coordinates relating to weather-map information fly by at a rate of about fifteen to twenty words per minute. We often taped the transmissions, decoded them, and ended up with an up-to-date map with highs, lows, fronts, and surface station reports. It is time-consuming to decode, but well worth the effort.

OCEAN CURRENTS

Currents are like rivers in the sea, and at times they had considerable effect on *Wind Shadow*'s progress. The equatorial currents became close friends of ours. They originate as spin-offs of colder currents in the eastern parts of ocean basins and gather energy from the trade winds. Their surface water moves constantly toward the west—just as we did. Their lift was always an important part of our calculations. In other parts of the world, currents are different—perhaps the most infamous being the powerful Agulhas Current off the East African coast. This particular gyre gives

➤ 127

rise to one of the most hazardous sea conditions known to mariners. "The current opposes the prevailing wind/swell direction and can cause waves of thirty meters in height." This appraisal is made in the traditionally conservative *British Admiralty Pilot*. Annually, merchant ships are broken apart and founder in the giant seas of this region. We were fortunate— *Wind Shadow* got through with relatively little incident.

The Gulf Stream is a lesser version of the same phenomenon, but the swells generated in the North Atlantic are not quite as venomous to vessels at sea as those of the Great Southern Ocean. Having sailed in both and sampled the effect of a frontal passage while in their grasp, I can attest to their reputation. Basically, the current impedes the progress of the wave train. A foreshortening effect develops and the seas take on a more vertical and less stable appearance. In the worst times, conditions in both the Gulf Stream and the Agulhas Current become untenable. Again, the best alternative is to remain outside their influence until a positive weather pattern ensures a more tranquil passage.

Local effects can also lead to strange weather phenomena. Ocean swells can be large and benign, while smaller, coastal seas can become quite hazardous. On *Wind Shadow* we encountered twenty-foot seas that presented absolutely no threat to us. They were long, rolling trade wind swells, spawned by a storm long since dissipated. We were also hammered by six-foot seas. Waves that would have been harmless in the deep-water realm became a real problem as we made our way into the Torres Straits, north of Australia. The strong currents and shallow bottom caused even small waves to stand on end. The relentless equatorial heat made keeping all hatches closed even more grueling. Finally we gave in and opened the hatch over the main saloon just a sliver. Moments later about fifty gallons of water poured through the hatch and found its way into everything from scrambling eggs to the two most comfortable berths aboard.

In our six years away on *Wind Shadow* I ended up with a pretty good understanding of the endlessly differing cruising conditions we met. I found this to be as critically important a skill as navigation itself. Physical capabilities such as anchoring, sail changing, and dinghy handling combine with this fund of knowledge to establish that all-important commodity, seamanship.

CHAPTER 6

Special Experiences—
South Africa
and the Indian Ocean

Time erodes many details. As the years go by the names of once-familiar anchorages begin to fade. Some memories, though—remarkable people and French Polynesian lagoons and palm-clad beaches among them—find a way to linger. Gales and other cruising traumas are hard to forget as well, but their recollection is tempered by the inevitable return of fair winds and sunny weather.

Each of the special experiences related here lingers in our family's several memories. Each is the creation of a unique time or circumstance. Other sailors in other yachts may find perspectives different from ours. Similar voyages in near-sister ships have yielded unexpected differences, because the sea and human nature abound with alternatives.

RUDDER PROBLEMS AND THE INDIAN OCEAN

A marine surveyor once described minor cracks on the starboard side of *Wind Shadow's* rudder as cosmetic defects in the gel coat. In the middle of the Indian Ocean his misevaluation nearly led to disaster. With difficulty, we limped into Port Louis, Mauritius, a small island thirteen hundred miles east of the coast of Africa. We had left Darwin, Australia, three months before and had sailed across the Indian Ocean toward South Africa. The near-catastrophe had begun two days before we reached Mauritius. Rudder vibration led to the discovery of the problem.

By the time we reached Port Louis the blade was attached only by

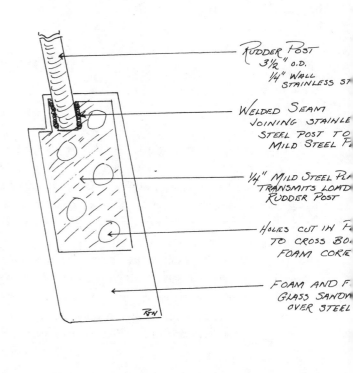

RUDDER POST
3½" O.D.
¼" WALL
STAINLESS ST

WELDED SEAM
JOINING STAINLE
STEEL POST TO
MILD STEEL P

¼" MILD STEEL PL
TRANSMITS LOAD
RUDDER POST

HOLES CUT IN F
TO CROSS BO
FOAM CORE

FOAM AND F
GLASS SANDW
OVER STEEL

A free-standing rudder like **Wind Shadow's**, *shown here, should gain most of its support from its internal structure. But* **Wind Shadow's** *rudder core, after outer fiberglass and foam had been cut away, revealed broken welds and an interrupted rudder post. In this cross section of an Ericson 41 rudder, notice the poorly designed junction of rudder post and load transmitting plate. Inferior quality welding further contributed to the potential for rudder failure. Such weak links in otherwise sound vessels must be remedied.*

threads of fiberglass. Upon removal and inspection once we were safe in harbor, I discovered that the builder had taken a life-threatening shortcut. He had saved on the cost of stainless-steel tubing by cutting the rudder post shortly after it entered the blade and improperly welding on a mild steel plate. These alterations seriously weakened the rudder but were hidden by the foam core and fiberglass encapsulation of the rudder blade.

Months before, in New Zealand, I had noticed that the cracks were more extensive than they had been in California. I wrote to the builder, indicating my concern and the serious nature of our voyage. His reply made no mention of the amputated rudder post and included a drawing depicting a tube that ran the full length of the blade. Reassured about the internal structure, I added additional laminate to each side and assumed the problem would be solved. We were lucky the repair lasted as long as it did.

It was difficult to fabricate a new rudder in Mauritius. Yves Betchel, the understanding owner of a shipyard and the benefactor to many ocean voyagers, allowed me to use his facilities. Neither resin nor fiberglass was available. A dozen cruising boats from all over the world gave me all the epoxy resin and cloth they had aboard. The shipyard welder was a fine craftsman and the ultimate result was, to our immense relief, a properly designed and built rudder.

In our five years of cruising I developed mixed emotions toward *Wind Shadow*'s spade rudder design. The semibalanced helm it created was easy to handle in all conditions. The self-steering vane operated the main rudder and seemed to like the helm characteristics as much as Lenore and I did. I have cruised and raced in many other boats and none has been easier to steer than *Wind Shadow*. Nevertheless, I realize the relative vulnerability of a freestanding rudder like hers. The 3½-inch-diameter rudder post was all that supported the blade.

After the reconstruction in Mauritius, I paid even closer attention to the rudder's condition. The bad weather en route to Africa and on the leg south toward the Cape of Good Hope had no effect whatsoever upon the new fabrication. Nor did the passage across the Atlantic and the two years of rigorous coastal cruising that followed. My conclusion was far from profound. A spade rudder is indeed more vulnerable than attached or skeg-hung rudders, but steering ease is one of its advantages. If that is the type of rudder you go to sea with, be sure it is well constructed.

To reassure those sailors whose vessels have modern spade-rudder and fin-keel underbodies, I shall here recount two of Fiji's many reef dramas. Both tales have happy endings, specifically due to the fact that the boats had a deep fin keel and separate rudder. The first mishap beset the forty-one-foot Van de Stadt sloop *Rebel*, for whom a minor navigational error became a major disaster. The vessel ran hard onto Mambalutha Reef, east of Suva, Fiji. She pounded on the surf-swept reef for two days until a tug finally pulled her off. She left the reef as she had entered, smashing coral each foot of the way. The fin keel saved her. It projected down far enough to keep the fragile turn of the bilge away from the coral. As it was, the abrasive coral ate through the 1½-inch laminate and two inches of lead ballast. But the spade rudder was so high and so far aft that it incurred only minor damage to its lower portion. An attached rudder would have been destroyed in this situation, and a shoal-draft or center-board vessel would have let the coral reach the hull. The vessel would surely have been lost.

Wind Shadow's similar but far less dangerous experience was also in the Fiji group. We had been pestered by a greedy islander and tried to leave an anchorage too early. The sun's angle prohibited our seeing the outer portion of Mulolo's unmarked reef. I was at the helm. *Wind Shadow* went aground with a grinding halt.

The tide was falling. We couldn't kedge ourselves off in time and were there to stay until the next high tide. I felt disgusted, and Tara and Eric showed no mercy for their father's dented ego.

Fortunately, we were in the lee of a well-protected cluster of islands. *Wind Shadow* settled into her coral niche and we pondered the problem. The crew of the seventy-foot motorsailer *Windson*, Jim and Cheryl Schmidt, noticed our predicament and anchored nearby to offer assistance. Jim and I set ground tackle, snorkeled about the hull to check for damage, and prepared contingency plans. If the wind switched direction (highly unlikely) or if a swell developed that might injure the hull, Jim would tow us off with his powerful GMC diesel. Conditions remained favorable and *Wind Shadow* floated free seven hours later. The heaviest damage was to the skipper's pride.

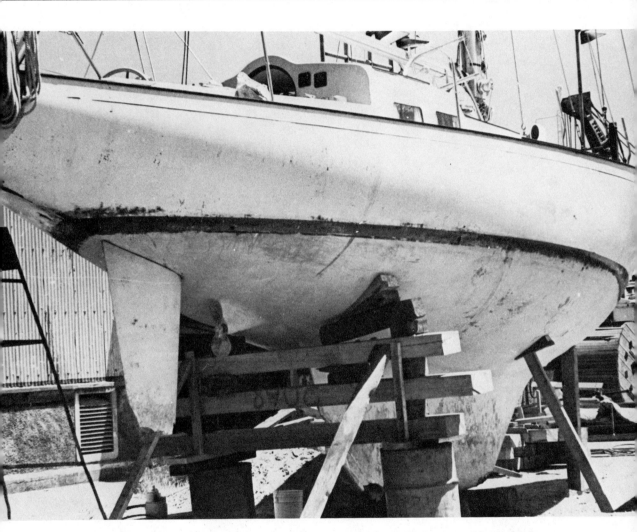

The sloop Rebel's *fin keel and separate spade rudder, shown here after her encounter with a Fijian reef, proved to be design assets: the keel took most of the abuse.*

Wind Shadow's grounding was less serious than Rebel's. The author took the occasion to paint the bottom, and the only real damage was to his ego.

During the wait I had a chance to paint part of the bottom as well as get a closer look at how a vessel sits in such a situation. Our deep fin keel was a definite advantage. *Wind Shadow*'s stern was high in the air and the rudder was well out of the way.

SPRINT FOR SHELTER

Simonstown is the name of a small seaport tucked into the lee of Africa's Cape of Good Hope. It is one of the safe harbors that small-craft sailors often make note of as they plan a passage south. We did indeed head for it in *Wind Shadow* following a gale-ridden passage from Durban, South Africa, south to Cape Agulhas. As it turned out, the weather was the least of our problems.

The Cape of Good Hope was originally named "Cape of Storms" by the Portuguese explorer Bartholomeu Dias, in 1486. As far as I'm concerned the name should never have been changed. During our two-month stay in Durban, I learned powerful respect for the intense cold fronts and gales that march across the African continent's tip. It was easy to see that our sail south could become the type of passage every sailor would rather avoid.

It seemed that the direct route around the cape was asking for trouble. Even in the calmest months, by Southern Ocean standards, the chance for heavy weather is significant. The best time for a round-the-cape passage is January or February, and even then only a few would attempt to sail from Durban to Cape Town nonstop. They try to take advantage of the strong southerly-setting Agulhas Current that has been known to add a hundred miles to a day's run.

Problems arise when a frontal system approaches with gale-force southwesterly winds imminent. Conditions in the current become untenable for vessels large and small. The cruising sailor has several options before the onset of weather like this. The best is to find shelter in a port, but there often isn't enough time to do this. An alternative is the old seafaring answer of heading offshore to ride out the storm in deep water. The effects of the current disappear. Waves tend to become less steep and there is more sea room for coping with the effects of the blow. If the cold front arrives before you have cleared the current, however, you are in trouble.

The next option is equally tricky—sailing inshore of the current. Theoretically this choice allows the crew to ride out the storm in the more tranquil countercurrent. Tranquillity is a relative term, however, and hugging what could easily become an unforgiving lee shore is a thrill seeker's gamble. Current conditions are indeed more favorable inshore of the Agulhas Current, but the coast's pounding surf and hungry shoals are menacing adversaries. It wasn't hard to decide that neither of these options was right for the *Wind Shadow* crew.

Ours could best be termed the "sprint-for-shelter" option. We decided to wait in Durban until January and then, very cautiously, harbor-hop our way from the east coast of Africa to the west. We would keep a close look at weather patterns and decide departures on favorable conditions rather than by calendar.

We knew that East London and Port Elizabeth are good ports to shelter in. Anchorages such as Jeffery's Bay and Mossel Bay, however, which are behind headlands farther south, offer protection in some winds but become treacherous lee shores after a shift. Getting away at the right moment is as vital as getting into shelter in the first place. The lovely harbor at Knysna, for instance, has a sandbar across its entrance that forms waves rivaling Sunset Beach, Hawaii. Seeking entrance or exit when the surf is up means a wild ride at best.

We made our way south from Durban with considerable anxiety. *Wind Shadow* avoided a gale by slipping into East London. We were a little late in our arrival at Port Elizabeth, though, and were well hammered by the second gale. With a sigh of relief we finally reached the commercial port. Coal dust and rust scale from steam tugs and locomotives nearby fell like snowflakes. In a day the decks and sail covers looked like the backyard of a New Jersey oil refinery. Nonetheless, the sheltered inner harbor of Port Elizabeth was for us the prettiest sight imaginable. Such are the dismal prospects for gunkholing about the tip of Africa.

Cape Agulhas, about three hundred miles along the coast past Port Elizabeth, is actually the southernmost point of Africa. We rounded the headland at night with bad weather at our heels. The prospect of facing a frontal passage at the Cape of Good Hope the next night was worrisome, but the legendary safe haven of Simonstown was within reach and if all went well we would find safe shelter by nightfall.

The weather somehow held off, and at dusk we slipped behind the Simonstown breakwater and headed thankfully toward the mooring area. We motored over to a South African Navy pilot boat at the entrance to identify ourselves and explain our intentions. We were courteously greeted and directed to an anchorage. Before long, with *Wind Shadow* safely tethered to a buoy and our "Cape of Storms" anxiety at last remote, Lenore decided to roast a chicken. Tara, Eric, and I were engaged in a serious Monopoly game. It is hard to describe the pleasure felt by a tired crew upon reaching a safe harbor.

This time the good thoughts were short-lived. Before the roasting chicken had progressed much beyond the lukewarm phase a call came from above. Someone wanted the master of *Wind Shadow*. It was the pilot boat again. Its skipper informed me that he had bad news for us. We were not allowed to stay in the harbor. This was a navy base, his commanding officer controlled the port, and "it was not open to yachtsmen."

Astonished, I drew his attention to the fact that we were surrounded by pleasure craft. He remained inflexible. I asked if we could slip the mooring and anchor south of the fleet. He informed me that the port jurisdiction stretched twenty-five miles in that direction and we must anchor beyond that. I asked what would happen if I refused to leave. He said I would be arrested. Eric heard the comment and charged below to get the spear gun, ready to hold off the boarders.

I recalled the Australian friend, a few weeks ahead of us, who had stayed in Simonstown. I brought the fact to the attention of the increasingly agitated pilot-boat skipper: "Why was our friend allowed to stay and we have been refused?"

"What nationality are you?" came his return.

"We're from the United States," I answered.

"That's the reason," was his final comment.

At that point, the memory of Penrhyn Island and our foolishness at leaving flashed through my mind. With an effort to stay calm I informed the pilot that I claimed my Geneva Convention right as master of the vessel *Wind Shadow* to seek safe anchorage. My crew was fatigued, bad weather was imminent, and going to sea would jeopardize their safety ➤ 137 and that of my sloop. I thought I was surely "headed for jail without passing Go." Instead, the pilot leeringly stated that he would report what I said to the commanding officer and would return.

Pleasant thoughts of a Monopoly game and roast chicken for dinner had perished. Lenore wondered if we should just set sail. We had been lucky in Penrhyn and had gotten away with taking such a chance. This time it was dark and we were exhausted from a sleepless thirty-six-hour passage around Cape Agulhas. I was not fighting for a principle here; I was trying to ensure the survival of my crew and vessel.

Eric had the spear gun and was ready to stand guard. Tara was asking, "Is Daddy going to jail?" every three minutes. While we waited for the pilot boat's return I made a single-sideband contact with a friend and explained the situation. Before our conversation had gotten very far, local interference made radio communication impossible. Whether it was intentional or not we will never know.

An interminable hour went by before the pilot boat returned. The skipper was completely unemotional. The commanding officer would allow us to stay on the mooring until 0600 hours the next morning. We were prohibited from going ashore or leaving the boat. We were to maintain a radio watch on Channel 16 VHF and to contact the port control at the time of departure. Before the last syllable of the last word had faded, the pilot vessel turned to port and steamed back to the dock. During the night the front passed through with all anticipated vehemence. Rounding the Cape of Good Hope in it would have been far worse than facing arrest.

By 0600 hours the next day the sun was shining, the barometer was up, and we were close-reaching toward the cape. I was quite confused over the previous night's encounter. South Africans had been some of the friendliest, most cordial people we had met anywhere. Surely it was an unlucky experience and nothing more. Months later, we discovered it might have been much more indeed.

In late September of 1979 there was a strange flash above the Great Southern Ocean, south of Africa. Satellite data and the response of underwater sonic equipment prompted the U.S. Defense Department to conclude that it was an atmospheric nuclear test. Allegations were made that South Africa and Israel had been jointly involved in the test. If that were in fact the case, the Simonstown naval facility would have been a logical staging point. Perhaps the tight security was a part of the international intrigue. It did seem strange that a vessel with "Cleared for all South African ports" on its papers should be refused safe shelter. Did we intrude upon an embarrassing military operation? If so, I guess the South African Navy finally decided *Wind Shadow* did not pose much of a strategic threat.

WILDLIFE OF THE VELD

Now that I have depicted South African officialdom at its worst, it is time to describe the brighter side of our visit. It begins with a mini-safari to the eastern veld and the Drakensberg Mountains. It became the shoreside highlight of five years of cruising.

The worldwide energy crisis had driven the cost of gasoline up to unheard-of levels. Our friends back home wrote despairingly of fuel costs exceeding the dollar-gallon barrier. In South Africa we faced a $2.60/gallon price plus rationing. No gasoline was sold on Sunday, the day we began our inland trip to the east coast's wildlife refuges, but fortunately our rented VW bug was economical. There were both problems and advantages to the petroleum shortage. Lack of traffic added confusion to which side of the road we belonged on. On the brighter side of things, at times we traveled for miles without seeing another car, and the sanctuaries were nearly devoid of other visitors. The guest log at the Umfolozi ranger station showed there were only four other people in the entire three-hundred-square-mile preserve.

I wondered if we would be let down by the game-stalking encounter we had so looked forward to. Thoughts of rustic signs pointing to the "Hippo Hollow Comfort Station" began to get me depressed. I worried that the paths would be overly groomed, that we would find a bureaucratically controlled outdoor experience.

There was no cause for worry. South African game preserves convey the authenticity of the habitat wonderfully. The large mammals blended into the surrounding veld; we never knew that herds of giraffe or a grazing kudu could be so miraculously camouflaged. Nor could we believe the ➤ 139 bulldozer strength of the white rhinoceros, returned from near-extinction as it is. Impalas and a dozen other varieties of antelope leaped warily through the thin brush. They were the target of predatory carnivores and had developed keen senses of hearing and smell. Tara noticed the gracefulness of the antelope, while Eric marveled at the stately warthogs. The days were a glorious educational lesson, never to be matched in any classroom.

In Mkuzi Reserve, we found a blind adjacent to a waterhole. The waterhole plays an important role in the lives of the creatures of the veld. During the dry season, April to November, it is essential to their survival. Predators realize its significance and await the arrival of their thirsty victims. The drama that we saw unfold kept Eric, a seven-year-old wiggler, sitting still and keeping quiet for hours.

First a family of baboons went through their morning ablutions. A wary herd of brindled gnu kept approaching and retreating. Apparently they could sense our presence. All about the outside of the blind flew small yellow weaverbirds. The males were busily constructing what must be the most intricate nests built by any avian species. The little creatures peeled thin strips of reed from cattails and wove them into an inverted-basket-shaped nest. A nest takes two weeks to build, we learned, and upon its completion the male seeks a mate. The more industrious of the species build several nests during the breeding season and raises several families.

At the waterhole a young baboon now wandered off to the edge of the muddy pool and was scolded by a rather large, dominant male. Something was being communicated. Moments later a bizarre-looking crooked-necked bird—a hammerkop—landed beside the waterhole near where the small baboon had been. The bird was large, about the size of a heron, but its neck and head were quite differently shaped. It too was acting very ill at ease. It must have spotted a lizard or gecko and was about to claim its prey.

Suddenly the hammerkop screeched as it was nearly devoured. Out of the shallow pool sprang a sixteen-foot crocodile. Its mouth was agape, snapping shut with the lethal swiftness of a bear trap. The hammerkop leaped astern with equal alacrity and missed disaster by only a few feathers. The eyes of all four of us showed our amazement, and we now watched the foiled predator wriggle its way back into the ooze of the waterhole's bottom. The water was no more than a foot deep, but all that could be seen of the enormous croc was a pair of nostrils and the bulge of two beady eyes. So now we knew why the large baboon had so vehemently castigated the youngster who had wandered off for a drink.

For several nights we stayed in a rondavel, a small hut made of woven grasses, inside the game preserve. The facilities were clean and dinner was served on a white tablecloth. As darkness set in, the veld came alive with the sounds of nocturnal animals. We sipped tea, shared our discoveries, and planned our adventures of the days ahead. Another game preserve, more looking, more wonder at the beauty and intricacies of the wildlife here.

INSIGHTS

Alistair and Davina Campbell are part owners of a sugarcane plantation in Durban. Alistair, whom we had never met, had relayed vital weather broadcasts to us as we made our way from Mauritius. At Durban we met the Campbells at last and found that the whole family also helps new arrivals acclimate to life in South Africa. They enjoy welcoming people until then known only by radio.

It was just before Christmas that the Campbells invited us to spend a few days with them. A few days became an unforgettable week. When we finally sailed away from Durban, we had found a warm friendship and gained some important insights into South Africa, thanks to them.

The wildlife of the veld was a lot easier to evaluate than the social implications existing in that country. We saw no sign of brutal oppression. There were, however, distinct barriers based upon racial origin. Cultural disparity between races compounded an already difficult situation. It is hard to establish common ground for an Oxford-trained economist and a Zulu princess with mud-stiffened hair. The former certainly has a better chance in the Western technocracy that is the South African way of life.

Alistair and I spent hours talking. The Pondo cane cutters on his farm each cut more than three tons of wet sugarcane daily. Their huts were simple and the corn-based porridge that was the staple of their diet ➤ 141 seemed unappetizing (as surely would our beloved canned Dinty Moore aboard *Wind Shadow* seem to them). The cane cutters worked for a dollar per day and a place to sleep and food to eat. The more money they acquired, the more they drank and fought. The cane knife was a lethal weapon and violence was part of their culture.

In the city, government and business power-structure positions were held by white men. Most workers were black or colored. It was of course impossible for us to condone a system that imposes restrictions like these. There is talk in South Africa of separatism and, at the same time, there is exploitation of a cheap labor force. It's the "work for me but live some-where else" ethic. My South African friends reminded me that things were the same in the States. They pointed out that we have both homo-geneous communities and those with clusters of the affluent segregated from impoverished people. I reminded them that financial segregation can at least be broken through.

"What if's" are great topics for night watches. Lenore and I later sorted out our feelings about the social situation in South Africa while en route across the tranquil South Atlantic. Trade winds seemed computer-con-trolled. For several days straight I had been able to varnish while under way. In the evenings, our dialogues were full of confusion. We tried to imagine the outcome if the aboriginal American Indian population had steadied at five times that of the European population, instead of being decimated as it was. It would appear that the white South Africans have done a more humanistic and skillful job of interacting than we apparently did. Reforms are taking place in South Africa and there is good reason for optimism about continued progress. South Africa is also stable, a trait alien to most other countries within the continent. The consensus arising out of the *Wind Shadow* South Atlantic Conference on Human Rights was like that of the UN—ambiguous. On one hand, we surely live in a glass house. (No puns meant, of course.) On the other hand, South Africa's racial barriers cannot be justified, but it is a stable, functional alternative to the despotic conditions in nations to the north. There, red flags, Cuban advisers, and Soviet aid are having more influence than all the Methodist missionaries who ever visited Tonga. Perhaps South Africa will come to grips with its de facto segregation problems. It may even develop a viable, mutually beneficial alternative. Only time can tell what is really best for this country and all its people.

FRIENDS AT THE DURBAN MOVIES

Sunday evening was movie night at the Point Yacht Club in Durban. We sat among fellow passage makers, discussing blown-out sails and steep seas in the Agulhas Current. We had met in other ports all around the world and looked forward to meeting in Durban if we could.

The main feature of the movie night was usually an outdated grade B film. It received the Academy Award from the passage-weary audience. I can't recall the name of that first Sunday night feature, but I do remember those we enjoyed it with. The crews of *Sunday Morning, Islander, Windrose,* and *Windson* sat nearby. These were people we had shared oceans with. Each crew had their own kind of cruising life.

We had first met the crew of *Windson* in Fiji, when they stood by to help us when we were aground on the reef at Malolo. Jim and Cheryl Schmidt cruised in a most civilized manner and their seventy-foot *Windson* reflected their pride in her. Radar, Omega, satnav, and a powerful auto-pilot were welcome aids, especially at times when Jim and Cheryl handled the massive double-ender alone. Two Onan generators provided power for the refrigeration/freezer system as well as for air conditioning and a video-cassette player. In the forepeak Jim's rather complete seagoing shop had gas and electrical welding equipment as well as a metal lathe for esoteric repairs. I recall that *Wind Shadow*'s restructured rudder includes special welding rod not found on the island of Mauritius, where we later spent time with the Schmidts again, but donated by the generous crew of *Windson.*

Tom Blackwell was also a partaker of Durban's Sunday dinner/movie night. Tom was seventy-four when we first met him and two-thirds of the way through his third single-handed circumnavigation in his big ketch *Islander.* We had been anchored in the lee of tiny Christmas Island, one of a few lonely outposts in the southern equatorial region of the Indian Ocean. When we returned to *Wind Shadow* after a long hike ashore, we ➤ 143 noticed a powerful, traditionally built wooden ketch newly anchored near us. She dwarfed *Wind Shadow* in size and probably could have kept a full crew quite busy. Her skipper was up scrubbing the decks and we exchanged greetings. It was hard to visualize such a boat being single-handed by a man well over seventy.

Tom had first sailed to Tahiti in 1937. He recalled a young man in Papeete who narrowly missed the chance to purchase the cutter of his dreams. The fellow laughed about his ill fortune and told Tom that now he would have to return home and make his mark in Hollywood. The man was Sterling Hayden, and he did just that.

Watching Tom handle the fifty-seven-foot *Islander* was a humbling experience. He shied away from the press. He underplayed the storms at sea and quietly went about crossing oceans. He enjoyed scrubbing *Islander's* decks with saltwater. His optimistic nature reflected the joy of sunshine, flying fish, and porpoises swimming at the bow. Tom liked sharing sea stories over afternoon tea. He knew he had an illness that would soon overwhelm him; news of his death in Durban six months later saddened all who knew him.

The first thing we knew we had in common with Mik and D'Ann Madsen, the crew aboard the thirty-five-foot sloop *Windrose*, was a profound respect for the Tasman Sea. Distaste might have been a better term. We had met about a year before in Sydney. Landfall at the Indian Ocean's Cargados Carajos Shoals was one special experience we shared with them. The shoals' prime attraction for us was the seabirds thriving there. We walked around the island for hours at a time and photographed nesting terns, noddies, and frigate birds. The isolation of these tiny clusters of sand and coral had kept human intrusion to a minimum, so the birds paid little attention to us. Mik and D'Ann Madsen now reside in Vancouver, British Columbia, their circumnavigation astern. But the recollection of those grand days ashore at the shoals must be as splendid for them as it is for us.

Charlie and Kathi Hast—with Jeff, Veronica, and Daniel—were another Durban-movies family who had succumbed to the daydreams of tropical sailing. They had built a fifty-four-foot ferrocement schooner named *Sunday Morning* and mixed the adventures of cruising with those of raising five children. Tara and Eric were always eager to see Veronica and

Tom Blackwell's fifty-seven-foot ketch Islander *and the Naranjos' forty-one-foot sloop,* Wind Shadow, *share the unusually quiet anchorage of Christmas Island in the Indian Ocean.*

The Hast family, movie-goers in Durban, South Africa, beached their wishbone schooner Sunday Morning *to paint her bottom.*

Daniel, their two youngest, who often joined us on diving expeditions. Sheli collecting and shark watching became part of our Indian Ocean routine.

Our two families shared potluck dinners in many harbors. One of the loveliest was near Fiji's small island Mbenga, southwest of Suva. Veronica and Daniel as usual had some new fishing and shell-collecting secrets to share. Several other vessels with good friends aboard joined us to catch up with news.

Just before dusk a large, professionally crewed ketch entered the lagoon and anchored a few hundred yards away. The vessel flew a French flag and had all the trimmings of a Mediterranean mega-yacht. Kathi and Charlie extended an invitation to the night's celebration. We assumed that the skipper and his wife would come by, once the afterguard was settled at dinner aboard the ketch. To the contrary, the Swiss industrialist who owned the boat also arrived, with his guests. They brought their version of potluck and the party carried on. The next morning we all went to a champagne breakfast aboard the ketch—a sixty-five-footer. Later that day we parted company—blue-water sailors aware of each other's lives. Since then Lenore has occasionally reminded me that life isn't too bad aboard a Swan 65.

CHAPTER 7

Tara and Eric

Tara, age thirteen—My father has promised that this will be our chance to talk about cruising. I am a good reader and am going to make sure that he keeps his word. We aren't living aboard *Wind Shadow* any longer. The boat seems lonely. Dad has even taken off all the bottom paint. It's sad to see our sloop on land.

I don't think my brother misses living on the boat. He's like most boys his age, all wound up over toys. Dad says that we are both going to talk with him about what will be written in this chapter. I like remembering about the places we have visited and so does Eric. He even thought the gales were fun. Actually we get along pretty well, even though he is a boy.

Eric, age eleven—My sister is thirteen and I'm only eleven. She doesn't really know as much as she pretends. I think she is the one that doesn't miss cruising. I build model boats, draw pictures of *Wind Shadow*, and like to hang around the boatyard. All Tara does is homework, then she calls her friend, Andrea, and talks about boys.

I can just barely recall living aboard in California. Falling off the dock is what I remember best. At the time I was playing "bounce" on the overturned Avon. It must have been tilted a little to one side. The next thing I knew, I was doing what the "swimming lady" called treading water. My father heard my sister screaming and quickly came on deck. He jumped in and pulled me out. It wasn't very cold. Dad sure looked funny with his dripping-wet tie and jacket. He wasn't very happy and I sure learned quickly about what I had to do to stay safe and dry.

Tara and I are beachcombers. I like to trap crabs and Tara is the best shell collector I know. We both learned to find the secret places where animals hide. Sometimes it was under a rock or inside some seaweed. We have searched the tide pools of rocky coastlines as well as sandy beaches.

ASHMORE REEF

Tara—Eric and I agree that Ashmore Reef had interesting tide pools as well as a beach to explore. Dad said that the islet was located in the Indian Ocean about four hundred miles west of Darwin, Australia. *Wind Shadow* had been nearly becalmed for many hours when we decided to head for the sand-and-coral reef. Eric and I were the first to see the island. Actually we saw a picture of the island. The blue reflection of the lagoon shone upon the white base of a cloud. We sailed toward the cloud and the island finally rose above the horizon. Dad says that the curvature of the earth is what prevents us from seeing low islands earlier. The chart showed that there was a narrow passage into the central part of the reef. My father climbed into the rigging in order to get a better look at the coral ahead. My mom was at the helm, Eric stood bow watch, and I kept calling out soundings. Entering such a pass can be very tricky because of coral heads that rise nearly to the surface. Everyone was glad to reach the deep, clear water of the inner lagoon. The wind had stopped completely and the ocean around us looked like a giant tide pool.

Eric and I wasted little time. We opened the locker and dug out the diving gear. We also brought Eric's small inflatable boat on deck. As he began to fill it with air, I recalled how he came to receive the toy. That memory brought me back to thoughts of French Polynesia. I recalled a day when Mom, Eric, and I had rowed ashore in Huahine. My mother saw an old cruising friend of ours and ran toward him, calling his name. A great reunion turned into instant embarrassment as Mom caught up to a total stranger. The more she tried to explain about her mistake the redder she became. Fortunately, the man was very understanding and that helped to ease Mom's chagrin. He mentioned that he was vacationing with his wife and son and would like to visit with a family that had

Small boat sailing begins with a rubber boat and a plastic sail. Here Eric runs before a trade wind breeze in Fiji.

actually sailed to Polynesia. That afternoon we had a good time aboard *Wind Shadow*. In the evening, we joined them for dinner at their hotel. They were quite interested in our sailing life. The next island they planned to visit was Raïatéa. We were also headed that way and invited them to sail with us. Plans were made to share the downwind daysail. Their son enjoyed steering *Wind Shadow* and, for a new helmsman, held a rather steady course.

Back to Ashmore Reef. It was nothing like New Zealand. It was uninhabited and felt very remote. Ashore we intruded upon hundreds of nesting reef herons. They squawked in protest of our visit. We had no intention of disturbing their rookery. A lack of footprints verified Ashmore's isolation. Along the beach lay hundreds of nautilus shells, cast from the sea by trade winds. The center of the island was surrounded by a ring of scraggly bushes. The middle ground was covered with thin, brown grass. Eric and I raced across the open, dry field. It always feels good to stretch your legs with a bit of running after a few days at sea. We noticed the shell of a giant sea turtle lying near where we had stopped. A bit farther away were two mounds of coral rock. My father thought they were probably graves of unfortunate castaway fishermen. Near the middle of the island stood a post holding a chart. It was written in a strange language. Maybe it had told the stranded fishermen the name of the island they were marooned on. A big tank to collect rainwater might have been a better object to install.

Eric—Tara and I went snorkeling at Ashmore Reef with Mom and Dad. We saw a lot of sea snakes. The yellow-and-black-striped animals didn't seem to belong in the water. Dad didn't think we did either. He made us get out just as he had done the time we finally got to see some sharks. Farther inshore we found good snorkeling, free from sea snakes and other pests.

Once I made a list for Dad. It began with what I enjoyed most about cruising. Lagoons with beaches like Ashmore Reef were my first choice. Tara and I collected shells, captured ghost crabs, and built castles in the sand. We knew that our stay would only be a short one. Dad had said that the anchorage was only safe in calm weather. When the trade winds began to blow we would again set sail. The next morning the wind returned. We carefully made our way out through the coral heads. Mom said it was harder to see beneath the surface now that the wind was causing chop. Tara and I stood at each side of the bow, Dad was in the rigging; each of us had a very important job.

GAMES AT SEA

Eric—At sea, Tara and I had special games we played. When we were four and six, we pretended that our Weeble-Wobble toys were pirates who lived on ships made of Legos. Mom's reading of the *Chronicles of Narnia* and *The Hobbit* added extra dimensions to our games of adventure. During good weather we did schoolwork on deck and hoped that a sail change would interrupt the spelling lesson. By the time we reached Australia, Tara and I were able to handle math, reading, and many foredeck responsibilities. Dad didn't call us on deck in gales, but he did give us more and more to do as our skills increased. At first I had trouble learning to tie a bowline. Dad tried telling me some riddle about a rabbit running into his hole. I always ended up with the rabbit climbing the tree and the bowline falling apart. Now I'm great with a bowline but I still don't like tying my shoelaces.

I hope I don't hurt Dad's feelings or ruin his book by saying this, but passages aren't all that much fun for kids. I kind of look at the long ones like I do Mom's vegetables. If I put up with them, dessert comes next. A new landfall can be better than dessert and a few passages were worse than a bowl of asparagus. I never worried about heavy weather. The feeling of *Wind Shadow* surfing down large seas was one of my favorites. Hot, slow ocean crossings and day after day of rain make me think that the best voyages are ones made in jets. If I think a little harder, I usually remember that the sun always did return, trade winds resumed, and the porpoises, again, played in *Wind Shadow*'s bow wave. Tara and I would lean over the rail and our friends would come by for a closer look. They were always happy and I liked sharing the ocean with them.

Some passages are like getting up too early on Christmas morning; time seems to stand still. Grandma says that Mom always used to ask the question, "When are we going to get there?" I guess I inherited her quan- ➤ 153

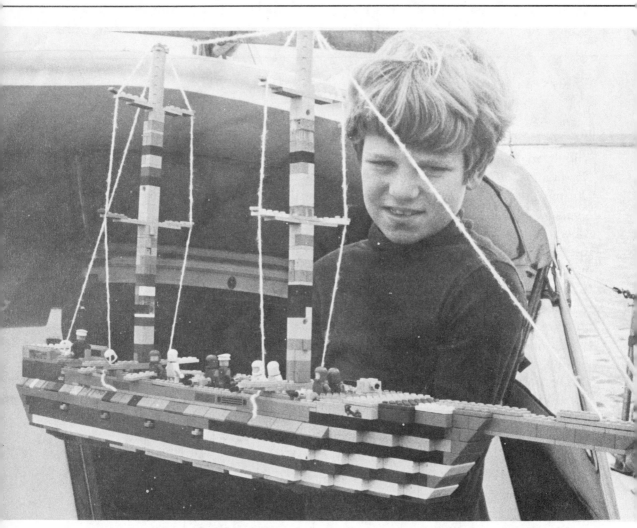

Whether for powerful ketch or stately castle, Lego blocks were favorite toys aboard
Wind Shadow. Note double-spreader rig.

tity of patience. Each afternoon Dad would mark our new position on the chart. In light air we wouldn't make much progress. I recall the disappointment of "twenty-mile" days. What made things even worse were the times when it was calm and Mom would decide to cut my hair. Watching hair drift westward at the same speed as *Wind Shadow* can be pretty depressing, especially to a kid who likes to get where he is going.

Tara—Even though my brother is a little impatient and likes to get where he is going quickly, he is a good sailor. He is also right about how similar a bad passage and a big bowl of asparagus can be. Time between departure and landfall can move slowly or quickly. It depends upon how the sea, the vessel, and the crew are getting along. My favorite type of day includes light-to-moderate trade winds, smooth seas, and sunshine. A good book adds the final touch. Hours of reading pass like minutes. We traded selections from our shipboard library with other cruising families. Good reading material was as important as good treats from Mom's galley.

BOSLEY, OUR SHIP'S CAT

Tara—One of the saddest days I remember concerns Bosley, our ship's cat. It took place in the middle of the Indian Ocean. We were sailing from Cocos-Keeling to Mauritius and had much more wind than we would have liked. Large seas arrived from many different directions. *Wind Shadow* rolled, bounced, twisted, and splashed over each wave. It was very warm, but all hatches except the main companionway had to be closed. I seemed to be getting seasick more often than ever before. Mom and Dad were worried about me and our ship's cat, Bosley. He seemed sick and very unhappy. Bosley was ten years old and had always been a part of what was going on aboard *Wind Shadow*. He often sailed with us in the dinghy. I remember when I was six and decided to trim his whiskers. We were living aboard in Channel Islands Harbor at the time. The trim looked fine, but it must have somehow changed our cat's sense of balance. The first time he tried to jump up onto the dock box, he was a foot too high and sailed completely over it into the water. Eric thought he was ➤ 155 a diving cat. Bosley was even more surprised than we were. Somehow cats know how to swim without ever being taught. My mom pulled him out, but we knew he didn't like swimming much after that.

Our cat was fooled again in French Polynesia. This time my dad was to blame. We were running out of the kitty litter that was used in his pan. Sand was an option; however, Mom and Dad had always made sure that as few grains as possible came aboard *Wind Shadow*. They weren't eager to start providing it for the cat by the bucketful. Dad says that when the need arises, ingenuity often saves the day. If he were a cat-pan designer I'm sure he would have patented his invention. He took a rectangular, anodized aluminum tray of cat-pan dimensions, scraped the inside bottom to roughen the surface, and poured in some epoxy resin. Next he sprinkled on kitty litter as if it were a graham-cracker crust to a cheesecake. When the resin cured, it looked like there was a nice soft coating on the bottom of the pan. Actually it was as hard as a rock and did not soak up any water. Dad used the last bag of litter in diminishing doses to convince Bosley of the authenticity of his new commode. Within a week he was accustomed to wearing down his claws, trying to move the contents of his synthetic sandbox. It was attached to a line; after each use it could be tossed over the side and towed until clean. Sometimes my dad is really creative.

Bosley was the best sailor in our family. He had completely adjusted to life aboard *Wind Shadow*. Since leaving California, he had never been ashore. In many countries, quarantine regulations are very strict. Animals aboard cruising vessels are not allowed to leave their boats. This is usually due to concern over rabies and other communicable diseases. Our cat became so lazy that prowling about on land would have been too strenuous for him. He was the most "laid-back" member of the crew.

The day he died was gray and overcast. Winds were gale force and waves broke into the cockpit. Dad put Bosley in a sail bag, tied diving weights to it, and buried him at sea like a sailor. It was hard to lose such a good shipmate.

Mr. Weber was a friend of ours from home who understood pets. He would often write to us, telling Eric and me what his dog and cats were up to. I'm sure he was sorry to hear of Bosley's fate. Mr. Weber was also the person most responsible for what became known as *"Wind Shadow's*

Log." It started as a duplicated letter written by the crew and published by Mr. Weber, the superintendent of the school district Dad used to work for. It described our travels and was also mailed to our friends and relatives. Eventually it grew into regular installments, featuring the adventures of our voyage. Mr. Weber not only understood pets, he realized how Eric and I would someday enjoy reading over the encounters we shared aboard *Wind Shadow*. We thank him for publishing the "Log."

GETTING SHOT AT

Eric—Tara says that since I'm so good at getting excited, I should be the one to describe the next experience. I was only four when it happened, so my dad will help with a few of the details. It was definitely one of our more scary encounters. It happened as we were trying to sail away from Kauai, Hawaii, headed for the Line Islands. Mom had noted that, on the chart, the waters adjacent to the Barking Sands Missile Range were a testing site and labeled "Restricted." Dad and I knew what to do. When we drew near the testing range, Mom called the range control officer on the VHF. She explained our intention and asked if we could sail through the restricted waters rather than around them. He indicated that there was no testing scheduled and that *Wind Shadow* could proceed through the control zone. About an hour later, we noticed a navy destroyer well off the starboard beam. It was steaming parallel to our course. A helicopter appeared from astern and things were really starting to get interesting.

The crew flew over us and waved "hello." At least that is what Dad thought they were saying. The destroyer was about a quarter of a mile to leeward when they fired. Tara thought we were hit and about to sink. It was only a blank round. Dad decided to heave to and surrender. He didn't put up much of a fight. Contact was finally made via the VHF and the misunderstanding settled. Apparently the range officer hadn't relayed to the picket vessel and the helicopter that we had been granted permission to enter the restricted area. We were allowed to sail away, unharmed but nervous. That was my idea of an interesting afternoon.

SEARCHING FOR TREASURE

Eric—Another interesting episode was our plan to search for Count von Lueckner's buried treasure. The count was part pirate and part hero. My dad told a story about him in another chapter. He sailed a square-rigged ship which plundered Allied merchant ships during World War I. His *Seeadler* carried an impressive arsenal hidden behind a false deck. Merchant ships would deviate from their course to get a closer look at the sailing masterpiece. Once they were within range, the count would greet their arrival with a few well-placed rounds.

A cruising friend of ours, Mr. Ahto Walters, met Count von Lueckner after the war when he sailed into New York Harbor. This time his ship was called *Mopelia* and there were no false decks or guns. Mr. Walters was offered a chance to sign on as crew. He passed up the opportunity. The details of the voyage of the sailing ship, *Mopelia*, are rather sketchy.

As *Wind Shadow* crew we tried our best to find out. Six days after leaving Tahiti, we arrived at the island, Mopelia. The remains of the *Seeadler* lay rusting on the coral before us. The atoll has a central lagoon and a current-ridden pass. Canted masts mark the locations of vessels that tried to negotiate it and failed. Strong trade winds enhanced the speed of the outgoing lagoon water. Under power and sail we made no headway. The worst part of the current lay ahead in the narrow pass. Dad saw we couldn't stem the tide. He eased back on the throttle, allowing *Wind Shadow* to flow with the current, away from the dangerous coral. Mom and Dad talked of heaving-to and waiting to see if the current would lessen. It was a dangerous area and we decided to forego Mopelia. Instead, we headed west toward Suvarov. It is hard to abandon thoughts of buried treasure.

In Fiji we again met Ahto Walters, the sailor who'd met Von Lueckner in New York. He had sailed his ketch, *Betty Lou*, to Mopelia. With good piloting and a bigger propeller, he made his way into the lagoon. Tara and I wondered, but never discovered, whether he had found the treasure hidden by the crafty "Sea Devil" of World War I.

EDUCATION AT SEA

Tara—Eric and I are all finished with what we wanted to say. We didn't say much about schoolwork, except that it was fun getting our new books and art supplies in different ports. We always received interesting letters from our teachers in New Zealand. We did learn many things about New Zealand that we wouldn't have otherwise. It's a good country. I guess my dad will finish the rest now.

Their father—One of the most regularly asked questions pertaining to our voyage is, "What did you do about your children's education?" The answer seems simple enough; we taught them ourselves. Getting into what was taught and how it was accomplished is more complex. The fact that Lenore and I each had a prior background in education was helpful, though not imperative, in the development of a functional primary-school alternative. The *Wind Shadow* approach is a viable one, but by no means is it the only way to cope with education outside the classroom.

There are a multiple of factors involved in the educational process. Some are creative while others are mundane at best. The primary-school-aged child needs basic skill development as well as abstract experiences. Engineering these into life on the high seas can be quite an accomplishment in itself.

Lenore ran the educational program aboard *Wind Shadow*. Prior to leaving California, she had acquired textbooks and materials from Tara's teacher there and from colleagues in the profession. Her intent was to develop a flexible, semistructured program that met both the children's needs and the constraints of living aboard. She and I agreed that reading and math should be the apex of the formalized approach. Social studies and science topics could certainly be dealt with in an informal, more spontaneous manner. The success of our six-year program can be measured in many ways. One of the clearest measurements may be that both children have adapted comfortably to the scholastic requirements of shoreside school. Tara is an honor roll student. Her brother earns Bs and Cs, and still feels Tom Sawyer and Huck Finn had the right idea toward life.

Certain other benefits of our *Wind Shadow* years are not directly mea- ➤ 159

Tara and Eric kept up with schoolwork under guidance of Lenore. Eric's concentration was sometimes less than model, but the learning did get done.

Watching a new coastline glide by, a favorite pastime, was another kind of learning.

surable and cannot be communicated on report cards. They lie in the realm of self-reliance, ingenuity, and genuine global awareness. This is not the time to dwell upon these. I'll refrain, for the moment, from leaving the three Rs.

At times teaching is a real drag. This is of course true in any educational setting and I'm sure children have the same attitude toward learning. Even though current educational rhetoric oozes with praise for individualized instruction, acquiring basic learning skills this way can give doldrumlike countenance to parent and child.

Lenore discovered something better than M&Ms to sweeten the prospect. She cut down time-wasting and focused on vital issues, figuring that two hours of productivity were more valuable than seven hours of captivity. When teaching and learning broke down into an adversary proceeding, it was time for a swim or a jog around the deck. We could be flexible with time. There's little interest in doing spelling when gale-force winds are punishing *Wind Shadow* and her crew.

As with most of cruising life, education at sea offers a few initially unseen problems. Some are easy to remedy if noticed early. Structure of lessons can be one of them. Adults can generally function in varying situations—some tightly controlled and others full of latitude, each eliciting a different response from the individual. Lenore and I found that Tara and Eric could also cope with differing degrees of structure. For reading and math skills, they clearly responded best to the rather formal approach we had decided on. Perhaps the formal structure was a less creative experience, but we felt that developing basic cognitive skills must precede the more valuable application of them.

Many New Zealand schoolchildren live on isolated farms and do not attend regular classes. Instead, they participate in the country's expansive correspondence-school program. Tara and Eric took part in this during the last half of our voyage. The program offered both the needed structure and interesting, highly motivating material. For three years our children learned to spell and speak the Queen's English. They learned about rugby, sheep farming, and Christmas pudding. When they came under fire for lapses in educational zeal, they'd remind their seagoing headmistress to avoid getting her "knickers in a knot." Despite the habit of adding u's after o's and holding the concept of Queen's Law above appeal, our children's Kiwi correspondence was unquestionably an educational success.

Not having a blackboard was a real problem. We had failed to recognize how important a learning device it was. When Tara and Eric returned to landside schooling, it was one adjustment that had to be made. Eric's fourth-grade teacher once had to declare emphatically that it was indeed story time and yes she was reading aloud to the class, but he could not come up and sit on her lap.

Story time had been a big event aboard *Wind Shadow*. Literature became a shared, delightful interest. Adventures, fantasies, and historical accounts were read to the crew by Lenore, oftentimes with all of us together in the cockpit, or, in the evenings, curled up in bunks below. Tara's reading skills flourished. Seven-year-old Eric discovered that he had not only his mother to read to him, but his sister as well. He became a great listener.

Still more of Tara and Eric's learning filled in peripherally—the special gifts of a cruising life-style. Staying with a Tongan family in Vava'u, or watching the first space-shuttle launching from ringside seats in the Intracoastal Waterway, were among these "lessons." Our family's love of the outdoors led to discoveries about fauna and flora. Together we snorkeled among the growing coral reefs of tropical lagoons, or observed vervet monkeys cavorting about the South African veld.

There were a number of things Tara and Eric missed out on. While they were swimming, diving, and sailing, their peers were immersed in competitive sports. Soccer, field hockey, and ice hockey today give them both challenge and disappointment because it's hard to start at the bottom level while your friends are already proficient. The summer's dinghy sailing does give them a chance to show their competencies. It's too bad that coaches and players tend to put less emphasis on participation than on success.

Who can really say what's best! The five-year-old at the skating rink who cried because his father made him skate may someday become a hockey pro. The child who has sailed across oceans may learn to design boats. Or perhaps he'll become the hockey player, and the tearful five-year-old may discover he'd love to take up sailing. . . .

* * *

164 ➤ *Befriended by a Fijian fisherman, Tara and Eric learn about the use of a fishing spear.*

Their mother—This is a wife's point of view about cruising with children. Many sailing and boating magazines publish articles about family cruising. This material offers all kinds of ideas about how to keep one's peace of mind in a rectangle approximately eleven feet by thirty feet, how to cook and clean up in a galley a tenth the size of most kitchens, how to assemble and stow food, how to choose clothes and toys for years to come, and what to do with children of varying ages on month-long ocean passages. For me, the answer to all these questions would be the same. The woman aboard must truly want to do what cruising and living aboard entail.

It is not easy to leave behind dishwashers, supermarkets, bathtubs, and lots of space. It takes time and practice to live, equitably, on a small boat. For us, our year of "practice" in California's Channel Islands Harbor let Tara and Eric become comfortable aboard and learn about their new environment. I learned how to use the galley efficiently. I learned what was really "necessary" for everyday life to be enjoyable—a gradual process of reducing material needs over an eleven-month period.

People we meet—especially other women—often ask me, "Would you really go cruising again?" This question is usually asked with a hint of the "poor wife who was dragged away" embedded in it. Much to their amazement, my answer is a resounding "Yes!" I feel that the experiences we shared—good, bad, and dangerous—were shared as a family, much like the pioneers seeking open spaces and new lands. Tara and Eric developed a self-reliance and individuality that is usually found in older children. Their transient life did not cause insecurity feelings to form because their environment, as a whole, traveled with them; theirs was a stable home life with all the same toys, sleeping quarters, and playing spaces. Their home took them from landfall to landfall, opening new learning patterns but never changing itself.

Because of our desire that living aboard be successful for us all, Ralph and I were very willing to forego much of what was "essential" in most households. I feel that our children, at age six and four at the outset, were influenced, in feeling and thought, by how Ralph and I felt. Our outlook was decidedly a positive one, and Tara and Eric thus felt no fear of their new environment or sadness in leaving their landside home for *Wind Shadow*.

Lenore returns from a trip to the market in Raiatea, French Polynesia, a treat of fresh French bread at the ready for dinner.

Ralph has mentioned the two worst passages we encountered—the Tasman Sea and the western Indian Ocean. It would be unfair to say that these storms did not affect Tara and Eric. They made them aware of the power of the sea and the insignificance of man; a concept hard not only for children to understand but adults as well. If these encounters had been too frequent, it would have affected their willingness and lack of fear in going to sea. But because we were so careful about when we sailed, and because we weathered each passage successfully, the two episodes did little more than disenchant all of us with that region of the ocean.

We spent six years, half of Tara's lifetime, living an unusual and very different life. Giving it up to rejoin the establishment once again was difficult. No longer do we worry about gales or rough seas. Our concerns have changed from ones of the immediate to ones of a longer term. To say that Tara and Eric were able to begin school and have no difficulty would be untrue. Even more than other parents, we must encourage Tara and Eric to learn how to fit into a peer group and help them in their struggle to cope with the "ways of children."

Their father—Tara and Eric had their fair share of trouble adjusting to life on land. I will always recall the day an inquisitive soul aboard *Wind Shadow* was asking me how our children coped with the dangers of life on a boat. At that moment Tara and Eric walked down the dock toward us. They were wearing shorts and T-shirts, clearly displaying that seven out of eight knees and elbows were covered with bandages. The woman looked at me with the expression of one viewing a child abuser. Hastily I explained that Tara and Eric were as unaccustomed to shoreside life as she was to boat living. In a matter of three days they had bruised and abraded themselves with their new interest in the terribly dangerous sport of bicycle riding.

The average child lives in a world of tight confines. Members in his peer group exhibit a latitude of behaviors influenced by what has gone on around them. Those who bring in new variables tread on dangerous ground. Tara tiptoed her way into what some call the mainstream. Eric plunged into its midst, totally unprepared. Both approaches had their ➤ 167 elations as well as disasters. Each underscored two yields of the cruising life—the grand flexibility of human nature and the cultural obstacles that trip up a child's efforts to get along with his peers.

It took our daughter a while to learn to giggle inanely, to babble and dwell upon the seemingly pointless issues that captivate many of her schoolmates. For better or for worse she has developed this capacity to an uncanny proficiency. Because preadolescent and adolescent culture in the United States today is less adult-directed than ever, it is probably to Tara's advantage that she so quickly mastered the skills of inane giggling and pointless discourse. She may in some ways, however, be hindered by the effects of long passages. Life aboard *Wind Shadow* had to be more practical than life ashore. Fashion had little significance, while the ability to fix a bilge pump did. Like the rest of us Tara learned to decipher the importance of an issue. Social roles aren't tested by reefs and gales. Tara's view of life around her is simply not the same as that of her friends.

Eric chose the other tack. He moved ashore and found that, in the summer sailing program of Seawanhaka Corinthian Yacht Club, he was a red-hot Optimist sailor who enjoyed wrestling with the instructors. He brought the same attitude to school in the fall and found that kickball wasn't the same as dinghy sailing and his fourth-grade teacher didn't like to wrestle. He was surrounded by children who cared nothing about diving in Fiji and lived a life he knew surprisingly little about. Classroom containment, desk sitting, and blackboard looking were hard rations for the foredeck crew. His teacher said he needed to hang out with some other boys at the roller rink. The PTA listed the establishment as "a drug-dealer's corner." We were concerned about more than roller-skating.

Having been a public school advocate for my entire professional career, I found it disconcerting to consider the alternative that we now pursued for the children—a private school education in the school in which Lenore was teaching. At his new school Eric's interest in boats, planes, rockets, and frogs is being channeled. He likes history, studies his spelling words and does well in math. There is room in his new fifth-grade class to be a sailor.

Reacclimation to the life ashore is difficult enough for the parents of cruising families. It is even harder for children who are unaccustomed to peer pressure. They must learn to stand back, survey the situation, and ad-lib. It is not an insurmountable task, and characteristics such as self-direction and a good sense of humor can ease the pain. But aren't these the attributes found in a cruising sailor anyway? Perhaps we'll all find that the problem isn't quite so awful after all!

CHAPTER 8

When It's Over

From the beginning of our cruise, landfall decisions and passage-making strategy had taken precedence in family discussions. During the voyage across the South Atlantic, however, islands and offshore sailing were secondary to a serious new concern. Lenore and I reluctantly acknowledged that the time to halt our cruising life was drawing near. Several factors influenced that acknowledgment. Tara and Eric were reaching an age where peer interaction was important. *Wind Shadow* was in need of a refit. Escalating living costs jeopardized our version of self-sufficiency.

We were all anxious at the thought of relinquishing what had become so significant for our family. The Caribbean became the last stop in our trade wind reach across three oceans. It offered a variety of experiences of its own, and hinted of the culture shock that lay ahead.

Wind Shadow was anchored in Salt Whistle Bay, the Grenadine Islands. We had just crossed the South Atlantic and being at anchor was something to appreciate. The southeasterlies were gusty, and I was on deck wrestling with a torn mainsail and skepticism about entering the job market. I was probably as employably obsolete as the hand-crank sewing machine before me. Each time I began stitching the seam, a gust of wind would try to launch the sail, sewing machine, and myself overboard.

Perhaps this is why I never noticed that someone had swum to *Wind Shadow*'s starboard side. A European-accented "hello" broke my concentration. The woman alongside asked if I had time to fix her mainsail. She was nude and I was trying to act nonchalant. "Um . . . er . . . I think there is something wrong with my machine," I stammered, not sure where to look. "Oh, it is only a small tear in a reef tie," she replied casually, taking hold of the boarding ladder. I went on to say how busy I was and I didn't think there would be time. Lenore, overhearing the conversation from below, called out, "Go ahead and do it, Ralph. That sounds like a simple repair. I'll help." With a smile and the comment, "I will bring it right over," the swimmer departed. Lenore asked how I could be so unhelpful to a fellow cruising sailor. I said, "Take a look out the port."

The ensuing sail repair was one of tact and diplomacy. Never before have I known a husband-and-wife team to work in such close cooperation. At the conclusion of our effort, I reminded Lenore of how right she had been; there is nothing more satisfying than helping another in need!

Cruising in the Caribbean was a different type of tropical sailing experience from all we had known. As in Polynesia, warm water and lush islands are bountiful. But over the years islanders have seen a steady stream of tourists and visiting yachtsmen; smiles are not as evident as they once were. The bareboat charter industry caters to those who flock to the islands each winter, ready to rough it in a civilized manner. Most have splendid vacations as they sample a Disneyland version of the cruising life. Itineraries of four islands in five days revolve about a menu of steak, lobster, and "Which restaurant tonight?" It is life in cruising's fast lane. The "dude ranch" approach to cruising is not like the life of those who cross oceans. Nevertheless, it must be an enjoyable vacation or so many people would not seek to do it.

I tried to recall such reasoning one morning at 0200 hours while a poorly anchored vessel drifted into *Wind Shadow*. As I tried to cushion the encounter with fenders, a woman in a bathrobe, curlers bobbing in her hair, arrived on deck. She announced that I had no right to anchor so close. I apologized and cranked in fifteen feet of chain. Her craft drifted aimlessly into Drake's Passage.

Several times we moved in order to avoid other such interactions. One episode is hard to forget. The congested anchorage inspired us to reanchor in the outer portion of the fleet. Three couples aboard a ketch-rigged, fiberglass galleon with a cliff-high afterdeck watched the move. I concluded the reanchoring effort by backing down on the chain rode to be sure the forty-five pound CQR plow anchor was well buried in the sand. I shut the engine off, waved a polite hello to the spectators aboard the ketch, and prepared to go below.

At this point one of the fellows in the cockpit asked if I knew that Captain Kidd had occasionally used this very anchorage. His navigator rallied forth with the comment, "Yeah, and he was probably the last sailor to use an all-chain rode like yours." His wife found his wit so amusing that she nearly sat on the hibachi. I was advised that things would be a lot easier if I switched to nylon. I was also told of the virtues of roller furling and quick-to-put-away sails, the lack of nightlife there, and the poor-quality roasts their provisioner had given them—how had I avoided a similar plight? I said, "Oh, we just bought lots of canned goods in Cape Town, and it smells like my wife has the corned beef and fried onions ready," and then I slipped below into another world.

We sailed directly from the Virgin Islands to the Bahamas. In George-town we were to meet Bob and Edith Melrose, cruising with their friends, the Huttons, aboard their ketch, *Lady Marion*. Bob had been my Sea Scout master seventeen years before, and although I hadn't seen him since, we had agreed by letter fifteen thousand miles earlier to meet in the Bahamas when the time came. Our three families had ten fine days together in the Exumas, snorkeling and beachcombing in these beautiful surroundings. When time finally came to head in separate ways, Bob and Edith invited us to sail to Greenport, Long Island, and use their dock as a home base for a while. This we gratefully agreed to do.

Wind Shadow enjoyed an easy reach from Man-O'-War Cay to More-head City, North Carolina. We spent a few days exploring Beaufort, entered the Intracoastal Waterway there, and meandered our way to Nor-folk and north. Our time constraints were flexible, and we thoroughly enjoyed the herons, egrets, and ospreys we shared each canal with. Travel in "the ditch" was captivating and made us look forward to a longer inside passage someday.

Returning to Long Island Sound began with a passage through New York City's very challenging East River. Swirling currents, commercial traffic, and close confines livened up the adventure. We were taking in ➤ 173

Tara and Eric view the Statue of Liberty as Wind Shadow *begins her trip up New York's East River. The two children have themselves experienced a special kind of freedom.*

Manhattan's towering waterfront when Eric spotted a huge timber dead ahead, just barely afloat. He called for a turn to starboard and earned even more esteem as an able crew member.

Through Hell Gate and on we rushed in the powerful current, and eventually into Long Island Sound. At the Port Washington Yacht Club, we anchored and basked in the welcome of relatives and friends. Here began a hectic summer of catching up on all that had happened while we were gone.

The Melroses' dock in Greenport did become our temporary home port. Aside from our having dockside electricity and the opulence of water from a hose, Tara and Eric had two good friends to play with. Eric and Davy Melrose were three and seven at the time, to our children's ages eight and ten, and both were as interested in catching crabs and playing in boats as were our own. Flounder fishing, swimming, and dinghy sailing became part of the day's routine. During rainy days the four adventurers headed for Grandpa Melrose's basement and an assault on the toolbox. Creativity blossomed and screwdrivers disappeared from their rightful places. On weekends we'd join grandparents, parents, and children ashore for a barbecue, to share the adventures of the week. I recall freshly picked Long Island corn and an abundant sailing dialogue as part of these good times. We will always be mindful of this family's welcome to us, which eased the sharpness of our return.

Tara and Eric by now had seen some of life ashore and sought to become a part of it. Fair winds and South Seas islands seemed remote. Friends and relatives bombarded us with "what will you do now" questions. We were out of phase with what surrounded us.

These were the thoughts going through my mind one midsummer day as I stripped the cover off the mainsail and prepared *Wind Shadow* for sailing. This time no ocean was to be crossed. We had become mini-celebrities and our adventures interested the hometown newspapers. We were taking a local reporter for a sail.

The reporter had never been on a boat before. A photographer had come with her, and they were ready to document our family and our trip. With a few misgivings, we got under way. Tara and Eric handled the docking lines, hanked on the headsails, and led the sheets aft. The photographer climbed aboard Bob Melrose's Boston Whaler and prepared to ➤ 175

Friends aboard the sloop Camelot *welcome the Naranjos to Long Island: Marian and Dick Hutton, Edith and Bob Melrose.*

After **Wind Shadow**'s *six years round the world, Eric becomes a ''tiller wiggler'' and changes from cruising sailor to dinghy racer.*

➤ 177

capture the action under way. Lenore took the helm and I set the main. Tara and Eric hoisted the headsails, and the reporter lurched at the first indication of heel.

A 15-knot breeze had worked its way in from Gardiner's Bay and *Wind Shadow* moved nicely on a close reach. Concentrating on sail trim and looking salty wasn't easy, especially when trying to answer the reporter's questions. Luckily, the photographer's needs were soon met and Bob was able to take him back to the dock when his film supply was exhausted. Now all we had to do was sail and answer questions.

The reporter must have been a psychology major. Her questions were complex and the most difficult ones would be posed during a tack or jibe. On one such occasion I was asked how I felt about depriving the children of a normal upbringing. At that point I asked Lenore to take the helm and cope with the questioning. She felt at home with it and I escaped the foredeck.

The laugh was on us, of course. The interrogation process had been intense enough for us both to miss spotting the red nun to port. A moment later *Wind Shadow* came to a halt while the crew kept on going.

"What was that?" asked the reporter.

"We have stopped for lunch," was my quick reply.

As Lenore gamely passed out sandwiches, I got the sails down and weighed the alternatives. I had left the dinghy at the dock. Unless I paddled an anchor out on my surfboard, there was no way to kedge off the sandbar. The folding prop offered so little energy in reverse that the prospect of backing off the bar was not promising. Calling Bob Melrose via the VHF might be even worse; he'd bring the photographer back with him. I envisioned a feature story: ROUND-THE-WORLD SAILORS SHIPWRECKED ON GREENPORT SANDBAR.

Casually, surreptitiously, the crew coordinated a plan. Tara and Eric changed the headsails, putting on the largest genoa and staysail. I positioned myself near the halyards. The wind was now about 18 knots.

Lunch concluded with an abrupt hoisting of sails, all sheeted in hard. *Wind Shadow* remained absolutely motionless, except she did slowly turn a little on her keel, assuming a more wind-on-the-beam position. Now at least her bow was aimed toward deep water. All we needed was a strong gust.

Luck was on our side. A heroic puff heeled us to thirty degrees, freeing the keel and launching *Wind Shadow* into deeper water. The sheets were quietly eased and we returned to a less dramatic angle of heel. Each of the crew tried to be as casual as our 130-beat-per-minute pulse rates would allow. The interview finally ended.

For two weeks we searched the paper somewhat fearfully for mention of the episode. Finally a three-page feature story rolled off the press. No mention of near-disaster was made; we had retained our salty image and learned to be very cautious about excursions into the limelight.

Once again Lenore and I met the financial cost of cruising through part-time work. This time we combined writing, dockbuilding, waitressing, and lecturing. It gave us some good insights into people and their ways of life. On some days I coped with creosote pilings while on others I dined with editors in three-piece suits. Lenore often joked about how stereotyped life had seemed as a teacher and how much her feet hurt as a waitress. One thing was clear, however. This wasn't Polynesia, the cost of living had risen drastically, and the ratio of necessary-work to cruising-time-available was at an all-time low. It was time to consider alternatives seriously, to begin the search for new commitments.

Down East seemed like a good place to start looking. It was early September, and there were a few fair-weather weeks left before we'd need winter shelter. Sailing on the heels of balmy southerlies we immersed ourselves in the seafaring traditions of New England. Block Island, Cuttyhunk, and Buzzard's Bay fell astern. We transited the Cape Cod Canal and arrived in Penobscot Bay, Maine. An old-timer said we were experiencing the best weather he could recall in over fifty years. Three weeks of clear northern sunshine convinced us he was right.

New friends introduced us to a refreshing alternative to suburbia. Maine's cruising grounds and woods reminded us of New Zealand. We felt at home in Penobscot Bay. Talk of relentless fog in the summer and squadrons of bugs in the spring only slightly tainted our view. We lingered and enjoyed good fall cruising.

Eventually, we worked our way back through the canal and followed the falling leaves south to Long Island. The approach of winter and lack of any compelling long-range plan convinced us to begin a passage south.   ➤ 179

The wish to spend Christmas with Lenore's relatives on Long Island complicated the issue, but we finally decided to sail to the Chesapeake and return for the holidays via train from Washington, D.C.

Christmas was a festive occasion. Unfortunately, it was also the coldest on record. On "Boxing Day" we returned to Spa Creek, Annapolis, to find *Wind Shadow* sheathed in ice. It took two days to get the engine started, but we had to do it or we'd have no more engine.

Central heating consisted of a wood-burning cabin heater mounted against the bulkhead of the main saloon, two trawler-type oil lamps, and a small kerosene floor heater. With all systems functional, the cabin temperature was eighty degrees at the headliner, sixty degrees on the top of the saloon table, and twenty-eight degrees at the cabin sole. *Wind Shadow's* waterline was surrounded by ice and we were worried that the Chesapeake would freeze.

To restore the spirits of the crew, Lenore roasted a chicken. At least that was her intention. After two hours the three-pound bird was lukewarm and she was sure the oven was broken. Further inspection revealed that the stove was so close to the hull that its heat was simply consumed by the ice around the hull. The menu was changed to southern fried chicken and things began to improve.

The next day we had the diesel purring away. I warmed the oil pan and the block by placing a can of Sterno and a cast-iron plate under the engine. The jury-rigged engine-room heater lessened the viscosity of the lube oil as well as the fuel.

Once all systems were operative, we began looking for our chance to exit the creek—but *Wind Shadow* could not break through the thickening ice. Even if her engine-and-propellor combination could have afforded sufficient power, which I was sure it could not, the damage that jagged ice would give the fiberglass hull would have made it a foolish choice. As the ice moved with the tidal current, we could hear the gel coat being chewed away. It was nearly as disconcerting as the sound of coral grinding on a hull. We stayed put.

After three long days, a combination of current, wind, and workboat traffic opened enough of a channel for us to make our way out into the bay. Sailing was bitter cold every day. It took us nearly two weeks to make our way to Norfolk (250 miles from Annapolis). During the day the

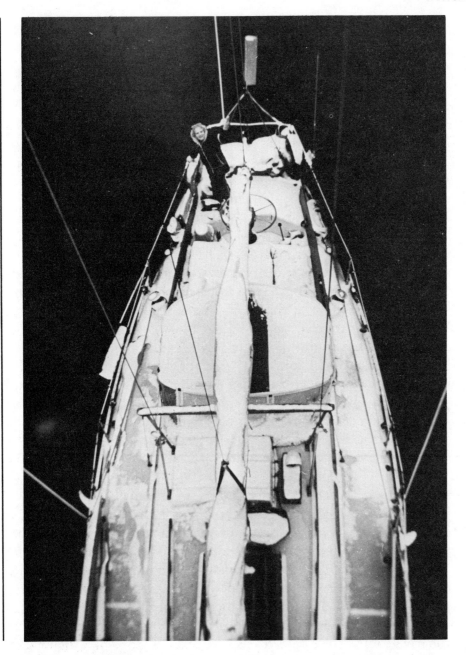

Snow and ice on the Chesapeake: shoveling the decks was a depressing prospect after a warm Long Island welcome.

spray froze on the deck and the hull began to ice up. Each afternoon we had to seek safe shelter in ice-free anchorages.

On New Year's Eve we sailed *Wind Shadow* into the Harbor of Refuge at the head of the Rappahannock River. It was dusk by the time we set the anchor. A gale had been forecast and reaching safe shelter seemed a blessing. Snow had been falling for several hours. The deck was coated. Ashore, everything assumed the same monochrome. At the water's edge, white gave way to the blackness of the evening sea. It was a Currier and Ives scene. When the elements are being experienced on such a firsthand basis, however, some of the aesthetics are lost.

Below in the main saloon it was a different story. Tara, Lenore, and Eric were preparing for a real New Year's Eve celebration. Cedar chips kindled a fire of well-seasoned oak. The odor from the wood-burning stove mingled with those from the galley. Warmth, good food, and the security of a safe anchorage were to the crew of *Wind Shadow* the essence of a celebration.

We unpacked party hats made by our New Zealand friend Christine Hall, to celebrate a Fourth of July in New Zealand. Lenore made a toast to the old year and its safe voyage from Africa across the Atlantic. The new year was welcomed with a bit of uncertainty. We were headed south toward Florida, the Bahamas, and either a passage on to Panama or an inescapable and major change in our life-style. But there was no confusion about *Wind Shadow*. She had carried us across oceans and sheltered us from the elements. We made our final toast to her; a splendid friend.

Ice, snow, and near-frostbitten fingers were with us all the way to North Carolina. By the time we reached Charleston, South Carolina, we had thawed out, survived being in the midst of target practice at Camp Lejeune, and recovered from a half-dozen episodes of running aground.

Our arrival in Florida led to a reunion with cruising friends as well as with relatives I hadn't seen in years. Good friends Carl and Jeanne Moesly, whom we had heard of for their involvement in offshore power-boat racing and had met in Mauritius, had returned from their second circumnavigation. Their *Rigadoon* lay at dock in front of a house they were building. Carl offered me a job working on his new home. I started in gladly.

A letter from Pop Melrose suddenly changed our tack. He mentioned that Seawanhaka Corinthian Yacht Club was looking for a boatyard manager. The club is nestled in an unexploited corner of Oyster Bay, New York, one bay removed from where I spent the first twenty years of my life.

At first flashbacks of ice and snow made me hesitate. But after some inquiries and very pleasant interviews I began to think that this might be a way of accepting a commitment ashore without completely abandoning the sea. I met with the chairman of the Boat and Yard Committee, Franklin McRoberts. We talked of ocean passages, S&S-designed sloops, and the concept of expanding the existing boatyard operation. I took the job. We would be back on Long Island by the third week in June.

Before going north we tried our luck with a mid-March passage to the Bahamas, but no good. A series of unpleasant weather experiences began with a northerly in the Gulf Stream. We got through another of those nights to remember and eventually found some shelter. After a disappointing week we sailed back to Florida, said good-bye to friends, and started what would become a rather slow trip north. A regular progression of cold fronts made an outside passage less than desirable. We followed the ICW through Florida and into Georgia, found a favorable pattern of southerlies and sailed offshore for Oyster Bay, but went inland again at Beaufort when another vigorous frontal system approached. Somehow the tiny Harbor of Refuge at the mouth of the Rappahannock River didn't seem quite the same as it had on New Year's Eve, just a few months earlier.

A week later, *Wind Shadow* sailed into the anchorage of Seawanhaka Corinthian Yacht Club. A cannon was fired, marking the opening of the 1981 yachting season and, for us, the end of our five-year cruise.

COMMITMENT ASHORE

At first we were solidly confronted by the "square peg in the round hole" syndrome, but eventually the *Wind Shadow* crew did reacclimate fully to life ashore. The pains of transition were eased because our new commitments could stretch to retain much of what we valued most. There ➤ 183 have been sacrifices. Even so, our values and attitudes have generally remained intact.

Where we live has a lot to do with what I'm talking about. I didn't have to succumb to the timetable of the Long Island Railroad. Nor did we sell the boat and immerse ourselves in a neighborhood with good streetlights and diligent crime watchers. I took over the operation of a boatyard. A gray cottage overlooking Oyster Bay became home. We sail aboard a variety of boats, have begun to refit *Wind Shadow*, and have introduced Tara and Eric to things they have missed. We have no television and appreciate the isolation of the island we live on. It is difficult to maintain values and attitudes so different from those around us. Our children are bombarded by contradictions. They have gone through a few aches and pains of adjustment but seem to have weathered most encounters.

About a month after we first moved ashore Lenore noticed that Tara's mattress kept sliding toward the wall. One evening she went into our daughter's room and found her pushing the mattress across the box spring. Tara told her mother that she had liked feeling the mahogany ceiling along the side of her bunk aboard *Wind Shadow* and moving the mattress against the wall helped her get to sleep. Today Tara's bed is in the middle of the room. She is an honor roll student and enjoyed playing a lead part in her school's musical. Her hockey coach says she is competitive and very team oriented. A year ago she had never been a member of a team or known how to hold a field hockey stick. Her telephone conversations seem unending and her overall acclimatization into the role of a normal thirteen-year-old seems to be going all too well.

Eric's interest in boats elicits a "that's-my-boy" attitude from his father. I will always remember his redesign of the Tartan 41, done at the Sparkman & Stephens offices on Madison Avenue soon after we'd ended our cruise. I must back up a bit to give the full perspective.

During our layover in Durban, South Africa, I completed an article on sail trim for one of the boating magazines. Several months later I received a letter from Roderick Stephens concurring on the value of the doublehead rig and suggesting an additional sail that later proved quite valuable. The letter ended with an invitation to my family and me to join him for lunch if we were ever in the New York area.

Perhaps it was putting on a tie again that made me nervous. My friend Bob Melrose didn't help at all. It was an America's Cup year, and Bob and I had discussed the boats and the crews. I am sure Bob thought I felt *Ticonderoga* would have made a good choice for the cup defender.

As Lenore, Tara, Eric, and I were getting ready for the pilgrimage into New York City to meet Mr. Stephens, Bob gave me one bit of demoralizing advice. He said, "Ralph, talk about cruising boats, rigs, and sail plans, but whatever you do, don't mention Twelve-Meter boats." His comments turned over in my mind during our trip to Manhattan.

As we walked toward the S&S office, I reminded Tara and Eric about their manners. Bob's advice also flashed before me. We entered the building and all my planning went astray. No sooner had we been introduced to the innovator of many modern yachting concepts than we were launched into conversation about *Freedom* and *Enterprise*. I probably sounded like a chicken farmer discussing thoroughbreds.

Fortunately, the conversation eventually turned to family cruising, and Rod's interests in our voyage flattered us greatly. After lunch, he shared several scrapbooks and a bit of the history of the firm with us. Eric was nowhere to be found. He had been looking over half-models and decided to sketch the profile of the Tartan 41. His efforts exceeded what would be expected of most eight-year-olds. Rod and his colleagues complimented him on the accuracy of his work. I felt proud indeed. Since then our son has been asking for a commission on each boat he draws.

Eric enjoys racing dinghies, riding bicycles, and avoiding homework. His mother often wonders about the mega-tonnage of the bomb that regularly explodes in his room. Eric does recall the clear, warm water of Polynesia, but that memory is currently upstaged by thoughts of how to acquire an Atari computer and what to do then, since there is no television to shackle it to. His best friend James also races an Optimist dinghy. He too is looking forward to the day when Eric has a new Atari, sails less, and ends up a few boat lengths astern. Whether that day will ever arrive remains a question to be answered.

LOOKING BACK

Human attitudes are said to be basically a product of people's surroundings. Occasionally the limits of these surroundings are a bit too confining, and perhaps this influenced our initial departure. Our voyage did give rise to some changes in attitude for all of us. We set aside a socially comfortable role and discovered the importance of self-direction, the value of time, some wonderful effects of being a family. As the crew of a small ship we responded to the sea as well as to the lands we visited. Tara and Eric learned that the skin of the planet they live upon is 75 percent ocean. It was a thin, invisible layer of air that interacted with the sun and the sea to give us calms, trade winds, and storms. *Wind Shadow* followed ocean swells and seabirds, headed westward through the heart of the tropics. Her crew learned about the flexibility of human nature.

Today we are ashore, though not quite entrenched in suburbia. Lenore and I discuss our chances for further cruising, and our wish for it. Our children are acclimated to the pace of their peers. The strength of their *Wind Shadow* memories will linger. The context in which they'll be viewed ultimately is hard to determine. Their friends say that they missed out on "disco" and "designer jeans"; or have their friends missed out on a chance to cruise the landfalls of the world?

It is also time to say something about Lenore. Blue-water veteran Peter Tangvald once said, "It's a lot harder to find a good boat than a good woman." Despite my regard for him, I disagree with Peter Tangvald's statement. The family cruise is essentially held together by the wife. A number of single-handers I have met would sadly agree. On our voyage I remember how Lenore managed to feed us so well without refrigeration, could row a dinghy with the ability of a true seaperson, and was willing to be hoisted to the masthead at sea to loosen a jammed halyard. A seafaring consensus between husband and wife, I gratefully acknowledge, is a cruising family's greatest fortune.

At times, now that we are settled into life ashore, Lenore and I wonder if future voyages will be limited to weekend sojourns on Long Island Sound. Will we find too comfortable a niche here? Or will certain values erode away before us and coincide with our desire to sail away again?

Refitting after return: Capt. Hanff of Hanff's Boatyard, Greenport, splices a new headstay for Wind Shadow, *part of getting ready for the next voyage.*

Horizon plans are always brewing in the minds of cruising sailors. We have learned how easy it is to part with couches, chairs, and other trappings of life ashore. Somehow a passage maker knows the right time to sail. If our time coincides with yours, may we both find a quiet anchorage to share the pleasures of a cruising life.

Appendix A

Other Passage Makers

The names of the following vessels appear in *Wind Shadow*'s guest log, in the order shown. Their crews shared anchorages and trade winds with us. It is impossible to forget the importance of these friendships.

Kirsten—U.S.A.
Tzu Hang—Canada
Whirlwind III—England
Cygnus—U.S.A.
Kalua—U.S.A.
Getel—U.S.A.
Topaz—U.S.A.
Morning Star—U.S.A.
Cara—U.S.A.
Yellowbird—U.S.A.
Castaway—U.S.A.
Faerie—U.S.A.
Banshee—U.S.A.
Content—U.S.A.
Sunday—U.S.A.
Nelly Bly—U.S.A.
Sunday Morning—U.S.A.
Cormorant—U.S.A.
Edward Richmond—U.S.A.
Rodonis—U.S.A.

Sunshine—Australia
Irish Maid—Australia
Preciosa—Norway
Bylgia—Holland
Altair—U.S.A.
Holokiki—U.S.A.
Sitisi III—U.S.A.
Irmelita—U.S.A.
Jahama—U.S.A.
Kaila—New Zealand
Bona Dea—U.S.A.
Freedom of Leigh—New Zealand
Aventura—U.S.A.
Saraband II—Canada
Constellation—U.S.A.
Assegaai—Australia
Ocarina—U.S.A.
Silmaril—New Zealand
Windson—U.S.A.
Decision—U.S.A.

Ravensong—New Zealand
Maudi-Marie—U.S.A.
Nunki—New Zealand
Boureen—New Zealand
Wanderer IV—New Zealand
Pieces of Eight—Canada
Kuaka—New Zealand
Mokena—New Zealand
Pippledoo—New Zealand
Dragon—U.S.A.
White Squall II—New Zealand/U.S.A.
Nimbus—New Zealand/U.S.A.
Rigadoon—U.S.A.
Cavalcade—New Zealand
Masada—New Zealand
Shearwater—U.S.A.
Caravela of Exe—England
Meisje—Australia
Betty Lou—U.S.A.
Sebathia—Australia
Ultima Thule—Australia

Farouche—Canada/U.S.A.
Intermezzo—U.S.A.
Wind Rose—Canada
Miranda—Poland
Aeolus—U.S.A.
Gillawa—Australia
Islander—England
Horizon—U.S.A.
Lou IV—Germany
Swan—U.S.A.
Yonder Ho—U.S.A.
High Pockets—U.S.A.
Lady Marion—U.S.A.
Jocko—U.S.A.
Dragnagle—U.S.A.
Sandpiper—U.S.A.
Windrose—U.S.A.
Flicker—U.S.A.
Small World—U.S.A.
Gladhval—Norway
Driftwood—U.S.A.
Solitaire of Hamble—England

Appendix B

Wind Shadow—*Hull, Rigging, and Gear*

Wind Shadow's voyage can be looked upon as an extended field test of both a boat and a cruising philosophy. Our outfitting priorities emphasized preparing her hull and deck structure, sails, spars, rigging, self-steering gear, and ground tackle for rigorous use. We also recognized the importance of a well-structured cockpit dodger, a stainless-steel propane galley stove, and dorade ventilators. Bilge pumps, boom gallows, and a secondary bow pulpit also proved to be worth the effort of installation. We did all our own work. It helped us to meet budget constraints as well as familiarize us with each system aboard.

A number of interesting observations have also been made about *Wind Shadow* since the conclusion of our voyage. For the past year we have lived ashore. I have had the chance to approach *Wind Shadow* as the manager of a boatyard, concerned with her refit. Lenore and I have disassembled our sloop and gotten to know just what effects forty-five thousand miles of cruising have had. The following comments name specific considerations and pieces of gear that were important to us, and show why they suited our sailing needs.

HULL AND FITTINGS

Fiberglass hull—Fiberglass proved to be an appropriate material for the kind of boat we needed. Removing through-hull fittings and ports and cutting away part of the cockpit sole revealed that there had been no ➤ 191

L/Overall	41'4"	Ballast	8,200
L/Water Line	29'2"	Displacement	17,800#
Beam	10'8"	Sail Area	715 sq. ft.
Draft	5'11"	C.C.A. rating	33.8 approx.

Wind Shadow is an Ericson 41: 41'4" LOA, 29'2" LWL, 10'8" beam, and 5'11" draft, with 715 square feet of sail. Wind Shadow's reefed double headsail rig proved to be an effective cruising sail plan.

tendency for any of the deck laminate to separate. Areas of balsa core and plywood sandwich construction were closely scrutinized. They had also fared well. The gel coat lasted thirteen years, five of which included the increased exposure to the ultraviolet radiation of the tropical latitudes. At the end of the cruise, the topsides clearly needed restoration.

I accomplished this through the careful spray application of Interlux's Interthane Plus. It rejuvenated *Wind Shadow's* white hull to a better-than-new status. Below the waterline, blistered paint and signs of crazing gel coat were remedied by stripping the paint, sanding the gel coat, and applying several coats of an epoxy primer called Interlux Barrier-Kote (#404–414). It sealed the porous gel coat and provided a good substrate for the adhesion of antifouling paint.

Through-hull fittings—Electrolysis and galvanic corrosion did some interesting things to *Wind Shadow's* through-hull fittings, heat exchangers, and most aluminum-to-stainless-steel junctions. All exposed metal surfaces below the waterline were electrically bonded; copper strap conductors lead to a sacrificial zinc and a milliamp meter monitors the current. The zinc usually lasted about a year and, I must assume, helped to prevent even greater corrosion problems. Even so, I felt it necessary to replace two through-hull fittings and associated sea cocks while in New Zealand.

SAILS AND RIGGING

Sail plan—Our prospective sail plan received serious consideration well before we found *Wind Shadow* herself. I chose a masthead, double-headsail sloop rig (cutter). I felt that it was a good combination of simplicity and versatility. The rig is nearly as efficient as a conventional sloop and much easier to manage. Some call the cutter rig a single-masted schooner. The foretriangle is broken into two parts, and the danger of being over-powered by a heavy number one genoa is eliminated. There just isn't any need for the sail; we sold the 160 percent, six-ounce genoa before leaving California. Our largest and heaviest Dacron headsail is a number three. When used in combination with an overlapping staysail, there is more sail area in the foretriangle than there would be with the number one. The advantage lies in the fact that neither of the sails is too large for easy

A light nylon drifter kept Wind Shadow *moving in even near-calm conditions.*

A single spinnaker pole improved the running trim of Wind Shadow's *headsails.*

handling. We carry a six-hundred-square-foot nylon drifter for light wind conditions. The sail has hanks and is easy to handle—under most conditions Tara and Eric can cope with setting and dousing it by themselves. When the wind picks up they get some help from the afterguard.

Stays and shrouds—The cutter rig is the most secure of all rigs: the mast is stepped near the middle of the boat and thus affords better shroud angles because of the increased beam. The inner forestay and running backstays add further support to the spar.

Runners are not as much of a nuisance as many seem to think. During periods when we had to short tack for a considerable distance, I often sailed *Wind Shadow* as a conventional sloop—the running backstays carried forward and tied off near the lower spreaders. I also disconnected the inner forestay at the deck-attachment point and secured it near a forward, lower shroud. *Wind Shadow* was thus returned and could tack easily.

Changing headsails—When weather and sea conditions are at their worst, a cutter rig is at its best. *Wind Shadow*'s reefing process is safe and simple, headsails could be doused or swapped for a different size, and the fore-triangle was not denuded of sail during the process. One of the two headsails always remained up.

This was an important advantage, because the remaining forestaysail or jib could keep the vessel relatively balanced. Our wind vane or autopilot was therefore not overpowered and the boat's motion was better. I prefer to move the sail plan's center of effort closer to the mast in heavy weather, and hanking the storm jib to the inner forestay had several beneficial effects. It considerably lessened the yawing caused by gusts, it kept Lenore or me from having to go as far forward for further sail changes, and the load on the spar was not transmitted as far aloft.

Slab reefing—I utilized a traditional slab-reefing process for the mainsail. *Wind Shadow* has a winch mounted on the boom to aid the operation. I usually added an extra lashing around the boom. It passed through the clew or the new set of reef points and took the load off the long jiffy reefing line.

Once two reefs had been taken in the mainsail, I considered how to reduce sail still further. After the small storm staysail had been set, the next reduction in area required dousing the main and setting the storm trysail. I preferred this to setting a third reef in the mainsail. When two ➤ 195

Steps running up the mast and the small rigid dinghy were worthwhile additions for Wind Shadow's voyage.

reefs weren't enough of a reduction, the wind had reached gale force. At this point I generally dropped the main, set the boom in a gallows frame, and hoisted the loose-footed trysail and sheeted it to the winch pedestal. I set up both running backstays and the rig was well supported.

Storm trysail—The storm trysail always remained bagged at the base of *Wind Shadow*'s mast. It reminded us of our Southern Ocean hysteria, a phenomenon we came to associate with the approach of each cold front. It always took awhile to adjust to the demands of a Southerly Buster. Our ability to cope with the wind and sea conditions was aided by having a trysail stowed in a ready-to-hoist position.

In New Zealand I had installed a separate track, parallel to the mainsail track, that rose to a point midway between the two sets of spreaders. Our new friend Christine Hall designed and made our trysail with the fierce Tasman Sea in mind; it was the size we had decided upon minus 30 percent. Seventy-two square feet turned out to be just right. Its luff stayed fully attached to the lower part of the quick track. We tied sheets to the clew and kept them in the bag too, so it was ready for hoisting and trimming. When conditions deteriorated, the trysail all too regularly proved its worth.

Roller-furling gear—I never felt a need for roller-furling gear on *Wind Shadow*. Under average trade-wind conditions, we carried a Yankee, forestaysail, and the main. If the wind continued to stiffen I would drop the forestaysail and tie it off to two lifeline staunchions. Although the sail was small in comparison to a genoa, its effect was startling. The operation was simple and there weren't any hard-to-replace pieces of gear. Roller-furling gear may offer the easiest way to handle sails, but it is neither foolproof nor gale-proof. There is much to be said for simplicity and the use of quality materials. Murphy was right; what can go wrong will go wrong, and it is likely to happen sometime between midnight and four in the morning. Having a genoa upwind in a gale can do more than ruin your night.

Refitting mast and rigging—Once we returned home, *Wind Shadow*'s mast and rigging underwent a thorough inspection and refurbishing. Two swage fittings were found to have hairline cracks. A strand in the headstay had parted earlier in our voyage and a lower shroud had snapped a strand in a gale approaching South Africa. I sandblasted and inspected the spar. ➤ 197

It showed surprisingly little sign of wear. I coated it with a prime wash etching solution, followed by the same epoxy barrier-coat primer I used on *Wind Shadow*'s bottom. A final coating of Interlux's Linear Polyurethane (Interthane Plus) added a durable, smooth finish. Standing rigging was completely renewed.

I also removed all other fittings and checked them closely. The tang fittings and clevis pin were noticeably free from distortion and frictional wear. I feel that *Wind Shadow*'s double-headsail, double-spreader rig was a fine choice for our needs.

ENGINE AND PROPELLER

Engine experience—The purist leaves his engine on the dock and then sails off, seeking adventure. The chances are he will find plenty of it, especially when he visits those tough-to-get-into, out-of-the-way places. For much of our voyage, *Wind Shadow*'s thirty-seven horsepower diesel had its share of problems. They weren't the engine's fault; they were the skipper's fault. I was a sailor and not an engineer, so each problem was new to me. I started with the basics, learning to bleed the engine, replace a pump impellor, and troubleshoot the alternator. The mystery of a diesel engine slowly unraveled for me, the hard way.

After the voyage, the 4-107 Westerbeke engine was brought into the shop and a thorough rebuild took place. If I had been as familiar with the engine during the cruise as I became during rebuilding, most of our difficulties could have been avoided. The smooth-running, four-cylinder engine—as opposed to the typical two-cylinder diesel—was a good option for propulsion in auxiliaries such as *Wind Shadow*.

V-drive and folding propeller—I also came to realize that the drive train is as important as the engine itself. Propeller design and placement are significant considerations: I cannot say that *Wind Shadow*'s V-drive and folding-prop arrangement is the optimum in efficiency and reliability. Perhaps I shall return to *Wind Shadow*'s original fixed two-bladed propeller. I've even entertained thoughts of moving the engine and reversing its mounting to eliminate the V-drive. Reliability becomes the byword to those

who count on an engine.

During our voyage, the power-plant installation and drive train left much to be desired. They led to a few dramatic failures, but fortunately never completely let us down under the most adverse conditions. Now that I have improved the installation and rebuilt the power plant, I am substantially more respectful of its merits.

Self-Steering Gear

Aries Wind Vane—Our silent partner deserves much praise. I have never met the owner and designer of Aries Wind Vanes, nor do I usually endorse products. Nevertheless, our pendulum servo self-steering system met our needs so well that special mention must be made. The model I have has gone out of production, apparently because it was made too well. The stainless-steel tubing and bronze castings functioned flawlessly. An occasional few drops of oil were the only encouragement the gear required.

Short-handed crew—The importance of adequate self-steering equipment varies indirectly with the number of available helmspersons, and we of course were shorthanded. Lenore and I found watch keeping much aided by our being able to leave the helm and trim sails, reef when necessary, or look over a chart. The Aries vane on *Wind Shadow* was able to cope with any sail combination. It didn't matter if I set the main and no headsails or a drifter and no main; the gear did its job. We were quite lucky to have such an essential piece of gear function so well. It was a pleasure to find such high-quality equipment available.

Ventilation and Protection from Sun and Spray

Dodger—A good spray dodger helps those below as well as the crew in the cockpit. Combined with dorade ventilators it keeps air circulating, even when hatches must remain closed. Tropical cruising necessitates good ventilation. The sturdy, well-reinforced dodger allows the companionway hatch to remain open in all but the worst weather.

Lee cloths—Lee cloths, lashed along the after lifelines, can add further ➤ 199 comfort to the crew's sea time. The lower portion of these cloths should be fastened with line that will break if a green wave hits the cloth. If not, there is good chance that the staunchions will break or be bent during such a situation.

Awnings—Awnings are important in the tropics. At first we constructed ours of white polyester material, thinking that would reflect more light. It did not stop enough of the sun's energy. By switching to a blue shade of the same material, much more of the light rays were kept out. The darker color did absorb more of the energy, but the fact that it had a better light-stopping quality made it a cooler cover. Perhaps material with white on one side and a dark color on the underside would be best.

ANCHORS AND ANCHORING

Ground tackle—We knew that ground tackle was important gear. I should have realized that a proper anchor-retrieval system was equally important. Instead, I had to discover it the hard way.

My troubles began in French Polynesia. I was sure that an all-chain anchor rode wasn't necessary and I felt that I didn't need a windlass and hefty bow roller to handle *Wind Shadow*'s forty-five pound CQR and fifty feet of ⅜-inch chain. In a calm I didn't need the equipment, and when there was a sandy bottom all chain wasn't mandatory.

However, many of our anchorages had coral outcroppings scattered within the sandy areas. When the wind began to howl, *Wind Shadow* would yaw to port and starboard, responding to a springy nylon tether. I had put buoys on the anchor rode, hoping to keep it above the bottom and away from the abrasive coral. Despite the buoyancy of the floats, the rode was pulled into contact with the coral.

At times it was imperative that we move before conditions became worse. Lenore would handle the helm while I hauled in the nylon rode and the chain. During each yaw to starboard, the chain jumped from the undersized fairlead. Once *Wind Shadow* was stopped dead by a well-buried anchor. My hand was nearly mangled by the jumping chain.

Upgrading the system—At that point I vowed to upgrade the ground tackle and install an adequate handling system. Both were accomplished in New Zealand. I purchased 250 feet of 10mm chain and added a stainless-steel roller fairlead as well as a powerful Nilsson manual windlass. The anchor could be dropped, retrieved, and housed in the fairlead without my ever touching it. The heavy chain rode minimized yawing at anchor. It was nice to be in our bunks and have confidence in the ground tackle holding *Wind Shadow* no matter what.

Our list of refit projects is still rather extensive. We have plans for lessening the size of the cockpit well, establishing an after berth for one of the growing children, and replacing a tired sail inventory. But the fact that we returned from a five-year voyage in *Wind Shadow* and knew we would keep her speaks for the fitness and durability built into our sloop. Transforming a well-constructed production boat into a serious passage maker is worthy of all the consideration and hard work her owners can give.